HERMENEUTICS: THE HANDWRITTEN MANUSCRIPTS

AMERICAN ACADEMY OF RELIGION
TEXTS AND TRANSLATION SERIES

Edited by
Robert Ellwood, Jr.

Number 1
HERMENEUTICS: THE HANDWRITTEN MANUSCRIPTS

by F. D. E. Schleiermacher
Edited by Heinz Kimmerle
Translated by James Duke and Jack Forstman

SCHOLARS PRESS
Missoula, Montana

HERMENEUTICS: THE HANDWRITTEN MANUSCRIPTS

by
Friedrich Schleiermacher
Edited by Heinz Kimmerle
Translated by James Duke and Jack Forstman

Published by
SCHOLARS PRESS
for
The American Academy of Religion

Distributed by

SCHOLARS PRESS
Missoula, Montana 59806

HERMENEUTICS: THE HANDWRITTEN MANUSCRIPTS

by
F. D. E. Schleiermacher
Edited by Heinz Kimmerle
Translated by James Duke and Jack Forstman

Library of Congress Cataloging in Publication Data

Schleiermacher, Friedrich Ernst Daniel, 1768-1834.
  Hermeneutics.

  (Texts and translation series—American Academy
of Religion ; no. 1)
  Translation of the author's Hermeneutik, including
Nachbericht by H. Kimmerle.
  Includes bibliographical references.
  1. Hermeneutics. I. Kimmerle, Heinz, 1930- II.
Title. III. Series: American Academy of Religion.
Texts and translation series—American Academy of
Religion ; no. 1.
B3093.H413   220.6'3   77-13969
ISBN 0-89130-186-0

Printed in the United States of America
1 2 3 4 5 6

TABLE OF CONTENTS

FOR ROBIN AND SHIRLEY

Schleiermacher: On Hermeneutics

by James Duke

The Art of Understanding

How is a text to be understood? How does understanding itself occur? These questions lie at the heart
of Friedrich Schleiermacher's theory of interpretation,
his hermeneutics. Fundamental to his view is the conviction that the first question can be answered only in terms
of the second, so that the notes and drafts of his theory
represent his persistent efforts to plot the relations between understanding texts and understanding as such.

Schleiermacher's Hermeneutics has been characterized
as a watershed in the history of the field.[1] Though he
drew freely from his Enlightenment predecessors, biblical
scholars and classical philologians alike, Schleiermacher
attempted a full-scale reconception of hermeneutical theory. Via Wilhelm Dilthey, especially, his influence has
extended far into the twentieth century, to Rudolf Bultmann and beyond.

Yet it was not until Heinz Kimmerle's edition, based
on a careful transcription of the original handwritten
manuscripts, that an assured and comprehensive overview of
Schleiermacher's theory of hermeneutics became possible.
The only other edition of the Hermeneutics had been prepared after Schleiermacher's death by his student and
friend, Friedrich Lücke, and this compilation was limited
almost entirely to a single lecture outline, the "Compendium of 1819," the second part of which was supplemented

by student notes taken during the academic year 1832-33.[2]
Kimmerle's edition, however, reproduces the full, incon-
testably genuine corpus of Schleiermacher literature on
hermeneutics. Omitting student books, it brings together
Schleiermacher's first notes, the so-called "Aphorisms of
1805 and 1809-10;" the several outlines prepared for lectures at Halle and Berlin; the two Addresses delivered to
the Berlin Academy of Sciences, and the marginal notes to
his outline jotted down in 1828 and 1832-33.

 The development of thought manifest in these materials is rich and complex. The reformulations of the theory
betray a restless spirit--restless first to master the
tenets of Enlightenment hermeneutics that they might be
recast into radically new form, and restless then to complete and perfect that new conception. A just assessment
of that development demands close study of the texts themselves. For the present it will suffice to point out some
of the key features of Schleiermacher's thought and to
indicate in quite general terms the significance of his
Hermeneutics for hermeneutical theory.

 Surveying the literature of his day Schleiermacher
identified three relatively distinct types of hermeneutics, bound to the service of biblical exegesis, classical
studies, and the law, respectively. He constructed his
own theory in dependence upon, or better, in debate with
the first two of these "specialized" hermeneutics. In his
opinion these specialized manuals provided little more
than an "aggregate of observations," that is, rules and
hints, gleaned from practical experience in translation
and exegesis, which were to obviate difficulties encountered in the study of ancient documents.

 In Schleiermacher's judgment such theories were not
only parochial and unsystematic, but, more importantly,
they failed to do justice to the actual goal of interpretation: to understand in the fullest sense of the word.
Previous theorists seemed content with a "less rigorous"
practice in their interpretations. They assumed that

understanding was proceeding smoothly until some obvious disruption arose. They would then resort to some expedient to remove the obstacle and pick up again where they had left off.

Schleiermacher concedes that, in normal conversation and reading, understanding does take place "as a matter of course." Consequently, a less rigorous practice may be adequate for simple, everyday matters. He cautions, however, that misunderstanding occurs just as readily, and the more innovative and complex the topic, the more likely it becomes. Genuine understanding requires effort and deliberation, in short, a "more rigorous" method of interpretation than that in vogue.[3]

Schleiermacher, therefore, proposes a fresh approach: a general hermeneutics which sets forth the art of understanding every linguistic statement, oral and written. This theory is to have both philosophical and practical significance. It would analyze the conditions under which understanding takes place and prescribe a method by which understanding could be achieved. The descriptive analysis is to undergird the method, and the method is to foster and enhance understanding.

To learn what understanding actually is, Schleiermacher directs his attention to ordinary conversation. There he finds operative, though virtually unheeded, two factors or considerations. There is a shared language available to the speaker and hearer, a "universal element," and there is a personal message to be transmitted, a "particular element." In actual dialogue these elements intersect, such that each complements the other.

A pre-given, shared language makes speaking possible. To convey a message, indeed, to think at all, a speaker stands under the power of language, subject to its rules and conventions and reliant upon its stock of words and concepts. The established linguistic system "allows" one to speak, and by the same token it channels and otherwise conditions one's pattern of thought.

Yet the message one thinks and articulates is one's own. It arises from one's own experience, one's perspective on the world, and one's special designs. Taking advantage of the flexibility and richness of language, each person forges a distinctive way of speaking that at once reflects and embodies one's thought. Thus, in an act of speaking, the pre-existent, almost inexhaustibly fertile and adaptable language is rendered determinate, giving birth to a specific meaning.

In keeping with this analysis of understanding, Schleiermacher's hermeneutics is to investigate these two sides of the same coin. Both factors, the universal-objective and the particular-subjective, merit equal consideration. For this reason, the theory is divided into three parts. There is first an introduction to general hermeneutics. The universal side is then discussed under the heading "grammatical interpretation," and the particular side under the title "technical" or, as it is later called, "psychological" interpretation.

In grammatical interpretation language itself is the center of attention. The individual author seems merely an occasion or case study for researching the nature and condition of language. The interpreter endeavors to reproduce the "sphere of language" shared by the author and the original audience and, with this in mind, proceeds to place each word, sentence, section, and work into the broader linguistic context to which it belongs.

In technical-psychological interpretation the author's command of language comes to the fore. In the "Compendium of 1819" the task is described as "the complete understanding of the style of a work." Here the interpreter is to penetrate to the peculiar message of a work by way of the author's distinctive use of language.[4]

In later notes this side of interpretation is subdivided into distinct technical and psychological sections, the former devoted to an analysis of the form and

organization which an author uses to present the message
and the latter to a consideration of the initial decision
or idea which impels the author to communicate. In effect, the interpreter is to trace the stages in the composition of the work, from its original inception to its
completion.[5]

Though Schleiermacher discusses grammatical and
technical-psychological interpretation in sequence, he em-
phasizes that in actuality they are inseparable and interrelated. Understanding arises from a deft interplay of
the two, and perhaps the constant revisions which
Schleiermacher undertakes are best seen as attempts to ex-
plicate that interplay in all its subtlety.

The word "interplay" connotes movement, and it is
striking how often Schleiermacher refers to the motion of
and within hermeneutics. To him understanding is a dynamic process, an on-going operation that proceeds more by
craft than mechanics. In addition to the interplay between the two sides of interpretation, there occurs within
each of the two a dialectical movement between comparative
and divinatory methods. The language and form of one text
are compared with those of others, and one author is compared with others whose works exhibit similar traits. But
comparison is not the whole of interpretation; indeed, it
is not even self-sufficient. The interpreter needs some
talent for "feeling" or "divining" how language as a living, organic power has affected the fabric of thought and
the mode of presentation. Also necessary is some insight
into the kind of person who writes in order to descry how
qualities unique to the author shaped the production. In
short, each method entails the other. They work in con-
cert to broaden and deepen understanding.

Certainly no metaphor for the movement in hermeneutics is more important than that of the circle. The hermeneutical circle, that is, the logically vexing proposition that the whole is understood from its parts and the
parts from the whole, means that interpretation is at base

a referential procedure. Though not coined by Schleiermacher, this proposition is applied at every crucial point
in his theory.[6]

Just as each word is determined by its position in
the sentence, so each passage and section of a work is to
be read in light of the whole. Yet each sentence yields
its meaning from the words it contains, and the work as a
whole is understood by working through its various parts.
More comprehensively, each work is to be seen in relation
to the totality of language. Yet access to the "language
as a whole" is gained only by reference to what is spoken
and written in it.

Similarly, each statement one makes must be viewed
in the context of that person's development. Yet that development is nothing other than the sum of the moments in
the person's life. For this reason the interpreter should
learn about the author's life in order to understand better what is meant. Yet it is by understanding a person's
statements that the interpreter comes to learn about the
one who makes them.

It is the "motion" in hermeneutics which in the final analysis makes it an "art." Focusing upon a text the
interpreter is suspended between its universal and particular aspects. Hermeneutics requires agility, an ability
to weave from grammatical to psychological side and from
comparative to divinatory method.[7] Furthermore, interpretation involves constant movement back and forth, for it
is always open to revision and supplementation. Since the
life of the language and the life of the person form an
infinite horizon, perfect understanding is an ideal which
is ever approximated but never attained.

Schleiermacher's Biblical Hermeneutics

For personal and professional reasons Schleiermacher
was called upon to deal with biblical hermeneutics, especially the interpretation of the New Testament. In the
course of his theological career he lectured on hermeneu-

tics nine times, once at the University of Halle and eight times at the University of Berlin. The premise for these lectures was that New Testament hermeneutics, as all other specialized hermeneutics, was warranted by and developed from the general theory of interpretation. The result is that the topics and issues treated in his New Testament hermeneutics, while derived from literature current in the day, are incorporated into his new framework. Thus when Schleiermacher takes from his Enlightenment predecessors the rule that the biblical texts are to be interpreted and understood in the same way as any other works, he relates it to his conception of general hermeneutics.

Schleiermacher believes that a specialized hermeneutics is justifiable on one ground alone--a distinctive language and content. Any work or body of literature may merit a specialized hermeneutics, so long as it represents a special "area of language" that demands special consideration in the application of the general theory. Consequently, New Testament hermeneutics is inserted into the general theory itself under the caption "special application to the New Testament."

The hermeneutical circle is set in operation to deal with the grammatical and technical-psychological sides of New Testament literature. The texts are to be considered in light of the nature and use of the Greek and Hebrew languages in the Hellenistic age and the special message which the authors sought to communicate.

Schleiermacher was convinced that Christianity brought forth a distinctive language and content. Christianity was, and remains, a language-producing power.[8] With Jesus Christ there came a new message or "idea" to be experienced and proclaimed. In communicating this message the authors of the New Testament thought and wrote in terms of the linguistic, religious, and intellectual milieux in which they lived. Their own understandings and expressions of their faith were conditioned by their heritage and environment. Yet at the same time they reshaped

or transformed, and at times even created, patterns of
thought and ways of speaking in accord with their new
faith. Thus the New Testament texts illustrate how universal and particular features intersect to produce a
unique literature.

　　Inasmuch as all of the texts in the New Testament
arise from the same basic "idea," they may be regarded as
products of a single "school" of thought. These points of
commonality are important. But they ought not be emphasized at the expense of the differences among the New Testament books. Each author wrote in terms of a particular
grasp of faith, and as a result each text reflects such
factors as its author's level of education, personal habits and interests, and relationship to the audience. The
authors wrote as they customarily did, and they assumed
their message would be understood by the normal means
available to their readers. In every case, however, the
authors wrote in order to articulate the meaning of their
faith.

　　Schleiermacher's New Testament hermeneutics is to
guide and aid exegesis. For this reason it delves into
many questions of concern to nineteenth-century exegetes,
e.g., the use of parallel passages, the notion of accomodation, the difference between literal and figurative
meanings, and the propriety of stressing or discounting
certain terms. Throughout, Schleiermacher takes into
account, implicitly or explicitly, the suggestions of his
predecessors and contemporaries. Here in particular can
be seen Schleiermacher's rootedness in the on-going tradition of Enlightenment hermeneutics, which devotes itself
to the free study of the canon and to the principles of
grammatical-historical interpretation. Amidst the welter
of detail, however, it is important to keep clearly in
view that the ultimate goal is to understand fully the
unique messages set forth in the New Testament texts.

Kimmerle's Interpretation of Schleiermacher

The Kimmerle edition of Schleiermacher's <u>Hermeneutics</u> appeared in the midst of a lively debate on the subject carried on within philosophical and theological circles.[9] Stimulated chiefly by the philosophy of Martin Heidegger, interest centered upon the primacy of language in the process of existential self-understanding and in the understanding of Being. Hermeneutics is linked to a phenomenology of human existence which inquires into the ontological implications of understanding. These concerns, associated as they are with attempts to overcome all historizing and psychologizing tendencies in philosophy, led many, most notably perhaps Hans-Georg Gadamer, to undertake a wholesale reassessment of the hermeneutical tradition which stems from Schleiermacher.

Kimmerle's work is clearly both a product of and contribution to this undertaking. It therefore comes as no surprise to see that in the introduction to his edition he strikes both contemporary and historical chords. The two harmonize, however, in a single thesis: a study of the manuscripts shows Schleiermacher shifted from a hermeneutics oriented toward language to one oriented toward the subjectivity of the author.[10]

Kimmerle believes this shift is manifest first in Schleiermacher's introduction to the "Compendium of 1819," though not carried out until later in the Academy Addresses and the marginal notes of 1828 and 1832-33. Whereas in his early period Schleiermacher sought to penetrate the content of a text by attention to its language, he later shifted attention to the process of composition leading from the author's original creative ideal to the actual finished product, that is, to the expression of that ideal in language. This shift is itself symptomatic of a more fundamental change of position. The earlier theory was predicated on the supposition that language and thought were identical; the later version posits a gap between the two, such that thought, as a purely ideal reality, is by

necessity modified when rendered in the form of empirical
language.

This thesis is at once revisionist and restorative.
Significantly, it is tied directly to Kimmerle's efforts
to publish a new, complete edition of the Hermeneutics.
The Lücke edition gave at best a one-sided picture of
Schleiermacher's thought. Confined to a single authentic
manuscript which was augmented by student notes taken in
1832-33, it was weighted decisively to the later Schleiermacher and his preoccupation with psychological reconstruction. The result was baleful. Posterity's judgment
of Schleiermacher came to hinge upon its opinion of psychologically-oriented hermeneutics. Those in favor of the
psychological turn, such as Dilthey, heralded Schleiermacher as a pioneer; those in opposition, Gadamer, for example, labeled him an exponent of the "questionableness of
romanticism."[11]

As revisionist historian Kimmerle produces a full
exhibit of texts to demonstrate that such conclusions are
miscarriages of justice. By making public the language-
centered hermeneutics set forth in the early manuscripts,
he redresses the injury and affords a more balanced and
circumspect judgment.

Kimmerle's restorative purpose, however, is to introduce Schleiermacher's "early" theory into the current
discussion on hermeneutics. This means that Schleiermacher critics should continue, but not stop with, their
complaints about subjective tendencies in his work.
Kimmerle himself moves on to other fronts, arguing that
Schleiermacher's preoccupation with pure understanding
leads him to abstract hermeneutics from its historical ma-
trix in two respects. First, his hermeneutics is detached
from the "special historical conditionedness of the object
it seeks to understand," since it relegates the interpreter's study of the linguistic and historical background of
the text to a preliminary and subordinate task. Second,
it is detached from the special present conditionedness of

the person who seeks to understand, inasmuch as it makes
"application," (i.e., the interpreter's interest in the
text and the text's relevance for the present) a second,
independent operation. In light of this critique, Kimmerle concludes that Schleiermacher "opens up a practice of
historical understanding which attempts to leap over historical distances," forgetful that interpreters are never
entirely free from their own situation.[12]

Despite these criticisms, Kimmerle is convinced that
much can be learned from the "early Schleiermacher."
Above all, there is the lesson that understanding, and so
hermeneutics, is to be aligned to the concrete process of
living speech. In his earlier manuscripts Schleiermacher
not only proposes such a theory, but makes considerable
progress in elaborating it. In Kimmerle's opinion it is
in this area that Schleiermacher's theory is of value for
contemporary reflections on hermeneutics.[13]

Kimmerle's edition, then, necessitates and enables
re-examination of Schleiermacher's hermeneutical theory,
with respect both to its internal development and to its
historical significance. This re-examination is still
underway, and in the discussion that follows only a few
salient considerations can be lifted out for comment.

As Kimmerle notes in a special "Afterword of 1968,"
his thesis of a shift in Schleiermacher's thought has not
gone unchallenged.[14] Indeed, attacks have come from two
sides. Since psychological considerations are present in
Schleiermacher's earlier manuscripts, it may be argued
that the so-called later position is simply an elaboration
or, at most, a shift in emphasis rather than in basic
thought. Conversely, since grammatical interpretation as
such and the objective-universal role of language is present in the latter manuscripts, it would seem that there is
greater continuity than Kimmerle suggests.

It is also to be noted that the nature of the source
materials once again enters into play. Internal evidence
for the alleged "new conception" must be garnered from the

Academy Addresses and from marginal notes. Can these materials be relied upon to demonstrate a new position? Granting that the Addresses touch upon the cardinal points of his theory, it is clear that, owing to their form and intent, they do not give an account of Schleiermacher's theory in its entirety and in its systematic coherence. For their part the marginal notes cannot stand alone, but must be referred back to the pertinent sections of the "Compendium of 1819" and the "Separate Presentation of the Second Part," that is, back to the outline of "early" Schleiermacher.

All this is not to refute Kimmerle's thesis, but it does justify a word of caution. The fact is that from start to finish Schleiermacher's hermeneutics involves both "objective" and "subjective" factors. The crux of the matter is whether he consistently viewed those factors as operative and manifest in language or whether he comes to set language as objective over against the non-linguistic or pre-linguistic thought of the author as subjective. Has Schleiermacher directed hermeneutics to the road leading away from the text, or does attention to the process of composition afford a better grasp of the text itself? Whatever the verdict, two distinct but related issues remain. First, what role do subjective-particularizing factors, linguistic or not, play in hermeneutics? Is concern for such factors tantamount to subjectivism and psychologism, with the result that they should be eliminated from hermeneutical consideration altogether?[15] Secondly, does not Schleiermacher force interpreters once again to consider how the relationship between la langue and la parole affects hermeneutics?[16] The answers to such questions will determine in large measure the future of hermeneutical theory, and by rights Schleiermacher should be a partner in those conversations.

Schleiermacher's Hermeneutical Legacy

A just assessment of Schleiermacher's place in the

history of hermeneutical theory must take into account his overall program. It would seem that to locate his contribution to hermeneutics in either linguistically-oriented or psychologically-oriented tendencies is to arrive at a half truth. In point of fact his theory is aligned to understanding as a global phenomenon, and so to all that that involves.

Schleiermacher's attempt to reorient hermeneutics was by no means fortuitous, nor wholly without precedent. It is reflective of the problem of understanding which streams below the surface of the Enlightenment and bursts forth in the romantic era. Thus it should cause no surprise to learn that Friedrich Schlegel, in that erratic fashion typical of his genius, adumbrated some of the signal ideas encountered in Schleiermacher's hermeneutics. Nonetheless, it was Schleiermacher, and not Schlegel, who envisioned and elaborated a general theory of the art of understanding.[17]

To found hermeneutics on the phenomenon of understanding indicates that understanding itself has become a matter of concern. It presupposes, or rather, acknowledges an initial difference or distance between persons: one wishes to communicate to another and the other wishes to understand the message. Yet this difference is not absolute, for it is mitigated by a shared language and a common humanity. Secured upon these two rocks, hermeneutics bridges the distance between partners in conversation.

Schleiermacher's theory also reflects a new relationship to history and to historical sources. Again, hermeneutics spans the distance between persons, author and reader; but these persons are now separated by the ages, by altered ways of viewing and relating to the world and by changed patterns of thought. For Schleiermacher, the historical text is not addressed directly to the present interpreter, but to an original audience. The present interpreter is to understand that original communication in terms of its historical context.

Schleiermacher has no illusions about the possibility of recapturing the message and its context in pristine form. Here, as always, the goal is to be approximated rather than achieved. But the mark of historicity lies in the loss of immediate understanding and of the taken-for-granted background of language and context characteristic of ordinary conversation. Historical understanding involves a detour. In it the original framework of communication is thematized and explored, opening up a dialogue with the past ultimately resulting in enhanced, critically-filtered present understanding.

This view of historical distance is related to the question of "authority" in both a narrow and a general sense. In the narrow sense the authority of historical sources refers to their normative status for contemporary life. In Schleiermacher's day this narrow issue of authority was joined in both classical and biblical hermeneutics. Classicists sought to recapture and rekindle the spirit of antiquity in order to foster the ideals of classical humanism; Christians sought to secure the normative character of the canonical texts in order to guide the life of faith. The realization that these texts arose in foreign intellectual milieux and that their contents must be grasped first in terms of their historical context goes hand in hand with a loss of immediate understanding and immediate applicability for the present.

In short, this narrow question of authority branches out into a more general but no less important one. To ask how to understand historical sources is to ask what claim they still hold on life. This question is the impelling force behind Schleiermacher's hermeneutics, and inasmuch as it is no less pressing today than in the age of Romanticism, his endeavor to answer it, now available in full, deserves reconsideration.[18]

To be sure, the field of hermeneutics has undergone considerable revision since Schleiermacher. Yet there is a thread of continuity running from Schleiermacher, through Dilthey, and on to Heidegger, Gadamer, and Kimmerle. That thread is neither language nor subjectivity per se, but understanding itself. Understanding is a mysterious phenomenon, yet known to all. It remains the central concern of hermeneutics. To orient hermeneutics to understanding has proved to be Schleiermacher's lasting contribution to the history of hermeneutical theory. By virtue of this achievement he can lay claim to the title of "founder" of modern hermeneutics.

The Text and Translation
by James Duke and H. Jackson Forstman

Schleiermacher did not prepare his manuscripts on hermeneutics in a polished form suitable for publication. Indeed only the two Addresses to the Berlin Academy were composed with public scrutiny of the text in mind. The other materials in this edition are outlines and notes which Schleiermacher developed for his own use in lectures at Halle and Berlin. Kimmerle's edition, supplemented by the emendations made by Hermann Patsch and approved by Kimmerle, represent a major stride toward a critical edition of Schleiermacher's handwritten manuscripts on hermeneutics.

This translation is to make Schleiermacher's Hermeneutics available for the first time in English. In addition to this Introduction and Kimmerle's Foreword to the German edition, it contains the following materials.[19]

1. Kimmerle's Introduction to his edition, in two parts. The first part describes the texts in detail and the second sets forth Kimmerle's interpretation of Schleiermacher's thought.

2. The Aphorisms of 1805 and 1809-10 (Ms. 1), with a loose page without date (Ms. 1'). These sentences and paragraphs are not truly aphorisms, but notes which Schleiermacher prepared for his lectures on the hermeneutical theories of the day. In this English edition

we have numbered the Aphorisms consecutively; in the
German edition they are unnumbered.

3. The First Draft of 1809-10 (Ms. 2), with a loose page
    from 1810-11 (Ms. 2').

4. The Compendium of 1819 (Ms. 3), accompanied by margin-
    al notes from 1828, and a Draft for the Presentation
    of the Second Part (Ms. 3') dating from 1822.

5. The Separate Exposition of the Second Part (Ms. 4).

6. The Two Academy Addresses of 1829 (Ms. 5).

7. The Marginal Notes of 1832-33 (Ms. 6).

8. Kimmerle's Afterword [Nachbericht], published in 1968,
    which includes a discussion of literature written in
    response to his edition as well as annotations and
    corrections to the texts noted by Hermann Patsch. Al-
    though the list of annotations and corrections has not
    been translated here as a separate section, remarks
    about the text have been taken into consideration in
    the translation and remarks about content have been
    included as notes to the manuscripts.

Though we have tried to be as complete as possible,
not all of the technical features offered by "critical
editions" could be included in the translation. We have
brought together notes from three hands--Schleiermacher,
Kimmerle, and the translators--and numbered them consecutively for each section. Schleiermacher's notes are
marked by the abbreviation FDES; translators' notes, by
the abbreviation TRANS. Those not specially marked are
taken from Kimmerle's text and his "Afterword of 1968."
All his remarks about content and meaning have been translated. Notes about the text itself, however, have been
omitted. In the first part of his Introduction, Kimmerle
discusses his own reconstruction of the text, explaining
that he indicated his judgments on incomplete and uncertain words by the use of brackets and single quotation
marks (' '). Since we have accepted his editorial opinion, these marks have been left out in translation. At
times we have set German terms within brackets in order to

clarify the translation. Moreover, we have followed Kimmerle's practice of indicating an illegible word by two
periods and illegible words by three periods. In sum, we
have translated the editorially reconstructed text without
often calling attention to the process of reconstruction
itself. We assume that scholars concerned with textual
issues will consult the German edition.

By their very nature these sources present both
translators and readers with certain difficulties. In
many cases the manuscripts are no more than repeatedly revised lecture notes containing numerous sentence fragments, clipped phrases, and bare topical headings. In our
translation we have made every effort to strike a judicious balance between textual faithfulness and stylistic
clarity. At times, however, we felt compelled to come
down on the side of clarity over literality. It was our
judgment that Schleiermacher's condensed style sometimes
called for restrained elaboration, and it seemed unwise if
not impossible to render cryptic German phrases or half-
sentences in "equivalently" cryptic English. When con-
fronted with the dilemma of making Schleiermacher more or
less clear in English, we chose to make him more clear.
In every case we sought only to state the meaning already
present in the German. Our intention was to make the
English version of Schleiermacher's Hermeneutics both reliable and readable.

The reader can hardly avoid some initial difficulty
in getting into the materials. At the risk of obscuring
the alleged evolution of Schleiermacher's thought, it may
be advisable to begin with the "Compendium of 1819"
(Ms. 3), and to move on to Manuscript 4, the revision of
the second part of hermeneutics, i.e., technical-psychological interpretation. Here the outline form used for
the lectures is most extensively developed and the topical
headings most thoroughly amplified. On the basis of these
manuscripts the reader can gain that "overview" of the
work, with its main line of reasoning and major thoughts,

which Schleiermacher considers essential for understanding.

      The other manuscripts may then be read and evaluated by reference to this mid-point. On the one hand, the two Academy Addresses offer a précis of Schleiermacher's "later" position, especially as he saw himself in debate with Friedrich Ast and Friedrich August Wolf, the leaders of the philological wing of hermeneutical theory. On the other hand, the remaining texts and notes illumine the course of Schleiermacher's development when compared with each other and to the basic outline of 1819.

FOREWORD TO THE GERMAN EDITION
by Heinz Kimmerle

The stimulus for the work which led to this edition
of Schleiermacher's Hermeneutics was a fervent, at times
tumultuous, discussion of the hermeneutical problem which
was carried on several years ago within the areas of the
humanities [Geisteswissenschaften] and theology. In the
course of this discussion it proved unavoidable to refer
back to the history of hermeneutics, for it was clear to
all that the present practice of understanding in the
sciences--and even in life itself--is determined by the
image of historical-critical research that developed in
the previous century. Again and again our attention was
directed to the position of Wilhelm Dilthey and to that of
his predecessor, Schleiermacher.

But the question remains whether it is sufficient to
read Schleiermacher's Hermeneutics, as is customarily
done, in terms of Dilthey and to see in it the bases
[Vorstufe] of Dilthey's theory of understanding as a psychological reconstruction, or rather, a re-experience.
The reflection on the phenomenon of understanding which
has emerged from several sides over the last few years has
put into a new light even the history of hermeneutics (cf.
Emilio Betti, Ernst Fuchs, Hans-Georg Gadamer, Ernst
Rothacker, and others).

This situation has occasioned a new edition of
Schleiermacher's drafts on hermeneutics that brings together his previously unpublished handwritten manuscripts,
and this work is not to be considered merely as a contri-

19

bution to the documentation of one period in the history
of this science. Rather, from the development of Schleiermacher's thought on the foundation of a scientific method of understanding which is set forth here, it becomes
clear that this "methodicizing" of understanding does dam-
age to its original structure. In the Introduction the
editor tries to show that the establishment of a scientific theory of understanding (in the sense of a general
organization of the processes of understanding according
to method) does indeed free understanding from its previous restriction to certain objects which alone are supposed worthy of being understood in this emphasized sense.
But it also leads to an all-understanding without orienta-
tion and to a separation of the process of understanding
from the acquisition of actual knowledge and from the application of what has been understood. As Schleiermacher
fashions his hermeneutics more and more into such a science of understanding, the connection of the process of
understanding to living speaking increasingly recedes.
The question of the discovery of the linguistic sense (of
the word in a sentence) shifts more and more to the question of what special (individual) thinking lies at the
base of a linguistic expression.

The editor thanks the Heidelberg Academy of Sciences
for the honor of including this edition in its series of
publications. For the substantative statement and treatment of the problem in the Introduction, he is deeply in-
debted to his philosophical teacher, Professor Hans-Georg
Gadamer. The Deutsche Forschungsgemeinschaft is to be
thanked for its help in making possible the studies of the
manuscripts in Berlin.

Villigst b. Schwerte/Ruhr, April, 1959   H.K.

EDITOR'S INTRODUCTION
by Heinz Kimmerle

The Available Manuscripts and their Reproduction

Schleiermacher's <u>Hermeneutics</u> has been published
once before as volume 7 in part 1 of his <u>Collected Works</u>.[1]
The editor, Friedrich Lücke, was a friend and student of
the author. In keeping with the approach which Schleiermacher himself normally took in his lectures on hermeneutics, Lücke entitled his edition <u>Hermeneutics and Criti-</u>
<u>cism, with special reference to the New Testament</u>.

In the Foreword the editor cited the following
sources: "first, Schleiermacher's ideas, as written in
his own hand, and second, several sets of lecture notes,
taken down in various years"[2] Lücke mentions three of
Schleiermacher's handwritten manuscripts, but he made use
only of the last, most thoroughly developed one. This
manuscript, forty-four pages long, comes from the year
1819 and includes, in addition to the introduction and the
completed part I (so-called Grammatical Interpretation),
the beginning of part II (so-called Technical, or, as
Schleiermacher also phrased it, Psychological Interpretation). The other materials which Lücke offers, some in
the form of interpolations in the manuscripts and others
as separate additions, are taken from the student notebooks. The two earlier manuscripts which Lücke mentions
in his Foreword are omitted. In addition, for Schleiermacher's later views the editor relies on the student
notes rather than on an additional manuscript from the
period 1820 through 1829 or on an extensive collection of

marginal notes from the year 1832-33. Lücke does refer,
however, to Schleiermacher's 1829 Addresses before the
Berlin Academy, "The Concept of Hermeneutics," (published
in pt. 2, vol. 3 of the Collected Works) as a necessary
supplement to the lectures.[3]

The present edition includes all of the materials
pertaining to hermeneutics from Schleiermacher's own hand,
but the student notes are omitted. Otto Braun's critical
edition of "Sketches of a System of Moral Philosophy,"
which also dealt with Schleiermacher's literary remains,
may serve as a model.[4] Accordingly, we present the pieces
in chronological order and reproduce the following handwritten materials.

I. The Aphorisms of 1805 and 1809.[5] This manuscript is sixteen pages long. Like the other published
here, it is the size of a normal textbook, and on a special cover it bears the superscription "On Hermeneutics
1805 and 1809." It consists of various aphorisms written
down while reading the hermeneutical literature of the
time, as can be seen from the numerous references and
allusions. In the margins of pages 3-7 there are notes
that were added later assigning each aphorism to the
introduction, first part, or second part of a work which
Schleiermacher was evidently preparing. The script, as
always with Schleiermacher, is very small and in places
quite careless and abbreviated.

To this manuscript we attach a loose sheet with the
heading "Example of Hermeneutics" (Ms. 1'), which also
appears to belong to this period.

II. The First Draft from the Period between 1810
and 1819.[6] This piece is seventeen pages long and a special title page reads "Hermeneutics First Draft." There
is no date, but the notation "First Draft" and the contents indicate that it must have been written before the
more fully developed treatment of 1819. The numbers inserted in the margins apparently refer to the successive
lecture hours. The manuscript includes the introduction
and the first part under the heading "Grammatical Inter-

pretation." We include a loose sheet, without heading or designation of year, the contents of which relate to the second part which at that time was always called "Technical Interpretation" (Ms. 2').[7]

Following this text is a four-page manuscript entitled "Application of Knowledge about the Author's Distinctiveness to Interpretation" (Ms. 2").[8] This represents the first elaboration of Schleiermacher's thought on the second part of his hermeneutics. In this manuscript, as in the "First Draft," the script is neat and clear. The handwriting on the loose sheet, however, is very careless, and there are many corrections.

III. <u>The Compendium of 1819</u>.[9] In the Lücke edition this manuscript was reproduced for the most part accurately and completely. It is entitled "Hermeneutics," and it is described above. We publish it without interpolation, although in a few places we have corrected and restored it over against Lücke's text. The manuscript consists of a series of theses which Schleiermacher elaborated in tiny handwriting, much the same as he had in his ethical sketches of 1816 and in the second edition of his <u>Brief Outline on the Study of Theology</u>.[10] On most of the pages of the introduction and first part, notes from the years 1828 and 1832 are compressed into the margins. We place the marginal notes from 1828 as footnotes to the text of 1819 since they always relate to definite passages there.[11] But the footnotes can be read as a whole, one after another, without any difficulty. The marginal notes from 1832 represent part of a new, more or less independent exposition of hermeneutics and so are placed in a separate section.[12]

The elaborations of the theses of 1819 are written clearly on the first pages, but they become larger and more careless, finally breaking off after the elaboration of the seventh thesis of the second part.

IV. <u>The Separate Exposition of the Second Part</u>, dating from the period between 1820 and 1829.[13] The

manuscript is eight pages long and is entitled "Second
Part, on Technical Interpretation." It is undated, but it
was put with the manuscript of 1819 by a later hand, and
according to that person's notation, it comes from the
year 1830. Nonetheless, judged by its contents it is simply a development of the second part of hermeneutics using
material earlier than that found in the "Academy Addresses
of 1829." Consequently, were one to date the manuscript
in 1830, one must assume a breach in the development of
Schleiermacher's thought. However, neither the student
lecture notes from this time nor the marginal notes of
1832-33 support such an assumption. The manuscript consists of a general introduction and an extensive treatment
of the first division of technical interpretation. The
application of this first division to the New Testament is
stated but not carried through. Moreover, the exposition
of a second division which had been intimated earlier is
missing. In the margins of pages 1-4 one finds the continuation of the final exposition of hermeneutics dating
from the winter semester of 1832-33. The entire text is
written in the form of a coherent final draft, although an
abbreviated style is used in the introduction.

V. The Academy Addresses of 1829. This manuscript
is seventeen pages long, but because the handwriting is
even smaller than in the other texts it is relatively
larger in bulk. The precise title is "On the Concept of
Hermeneutics, with reference to F. A. Wolf's Instructions
and Ast's Textbook."

Actually, this manuscript is comprised of two papers
which Schleiermacher read before plenary sessions of the
Prussian Academy of Sciences on August 13 and October 22,
1829. We learn this from the minutes of the Academy as
well as from a notation by Ludwig Jonas in the margin of
the manuscript. The two papers were published as number 4
of group V "On Philology" in volume 3, Speeches and
Papers, in part III of Schleiermacher's Collected Works.
The minutes of the Academy show that both papers were

originally scheduled for presentation to the philosophi-
cal-historical section of the Academy and that on short
notice it was decided that they should be read before the
entire Academy. This accounts for the special form of the
presentations and Schleiermacher's own dating. Evidently,
the topic was first developed for presentation to the section meeting, since its first form exhibits a direct, personally colored mode of treatment. According to Schleiermacher's record, the first lecture was scheduled for
August 12 and the second was projected for some time in
October. After the addresses were re-scheduled for presentation to the entire Academy, Schleiermacher reworked
them and added numerous corrections and marginal notes to
give them a more scientific and objective character. We
offer the final redaction in this edition, but we clearly
indicate where changes or insertions were made. From the
notes the reader can restore the first draft, which in
many respects is very interesting.[14]

VI. <u>The Marginal Notes of 1832-33</u>. As we have already noted, Schleiermacher had made comprehensive notes
for his last series of lectures on hermeneutics. Those
for the introduction and first part were written down in
the margins of the "<u>Compendium of 1819</u>," and those for the
second part were set in the margin of the "<u>Separate Expo-
sition</u>" of that part (Ms. 4). These notes represent a
new, continuous exposition which only occasionally related
directly to the earlier notes. Therefore, we reproduce
these marginal notes as an independent text and we must
ask the reader to look up the few direct references to the
passages which Schleiermacher designates.

All of these manuscripts are located in the collection of Schleiermacher's literary remains in the <u>Archiv
des Instituts für deutsche Sprache und Literatur der
Wissenschaften</u> (Berlin, Unter den Linden 8). Manuscripts
1-4 and 6 are in the archival box titled "Hermeneutics,"
whereas Manuscript 5 is in the case titled "Academica."

In this edition we retain Schleiermacher's orthogra-
phy and his punctuation.[15] Abbreviated words have been

completed, and the added letters have been set inside
brackets (except for standard and recurrent abbreviations
common to that period). Occasionally punctuation marks or
individual words are also inserted into the text, especially where the sense clearly demands it and where it
seems that Schleiermacher had merely forgotten to write
the sign or words. These insertions, too, are enclosed by
brackets. Where a word is illegible two periods have been
printed; three periods are used where several words in a
row are illegible. Where the reading of a word remains
uncertain it is enclosed by single quotation marks (' ').

After careful consideration, the manuscripts on the
theme "Criticism," also contained in the archival box labeled "Hermeneutics," have been left out. On the one
hand, these manuscripts are not sufficiently developed to
be suitable for publication. Lücke did not use them
either, and in his Foreword he rightly explains: "Unfortunately, only six or seven pages from various times have
been found dealing with criticism. They are repeated beginnings, hastily and carelessly written, and at times
only short sentences and notes."[16] On the other hand, a
separate edition of the hermeneutical sketches seems justified by virtue of the subject matter itself, for the
development of Schleiermacher's thought about hermeneutics
shows that these materials represent an important theme in
terms of his overall thought. In the second section of
this Introduction we try to show how for Schleiermacher
hermeneutics comes more and more to gain a philosophical
status and how it assumes an important place in his speculative system. This cannot be said at all about philological criticism. To be sure, in the paper he presented to
the Academy in 1830 on "The Concept and Arrangement of
Philological Criticism," Schleiermacher brought this discipline into closer relation to hermeneutics. Nonetheless, it clearly turns out to be a subordinate activity
which comes into being only "in connection with the diffi-

culties with which hermeneutics feels itself confined."
And although philological criticism comes first in point
of time, it only supports actual hermeneutics and secures
an authentic text for hermeneutical application.[17]

The Development of Schleiermacher's
Thought on Hermeneutics

The philosophy of Schleiermacher achieved its historical impact primarily through the mediation of Wilhelm
Dilthey. Dilthey's essay of 1900 on "The Origin of Hermeneutics," which closed with a description of Schleiermacher's conception, has been of decisive significance for
the understanding of Schleiermacher since that time.[18]
Rudolf Odebrecht, for example, so thoroughly accepts
Dilthey's analysis that he can write in the Introduction
to the new edition of Schleiermacher's Dialektik: "After
Dilthey's instructive essay on the merits of Schleiermacher it is unnecessary to discuss further the foundation
of a philosophical art of interpretation."[19] In his essay
on "The Problem of Hermeneutics" Rudolf Bultmann also
looks at Schleiermacher through Dilthey's eyes and assumes that the two men held to a common fundamental position.[20]

But the study of the handwritten manuscripts shows
that Dilthey's interpretation holds at best for the very
latest conception of Schleiermacher, as it is stated in
the introduction of the 1819 manuscript and is then carried through in the 1829 Addresses to the Academy and in
the final lectures of 1832-33. On the basis of his fragmentary materials, understanding seemed to Dilthey to consist in the conception, which Dilthey took over from his
predecessors and assumed to be correct, of "psychological
reconstruction" which is directed toward the "creative
process" of the origin of a work.[21] The emphasis, especially in the earlier manuscripts but also right up to the
last, that Schleiermacher gives to grammatical interpretation and to the understanding of language developed there-

in is not properly recognized. Furthermore, the development of Schleiermacher's thinking, the general trend of
which is indicated by the internal contradictions of the
statements of 1819, is not taken into account at all.
Thus it is necessary to interpret Schleiermacher's hermeneutics anew, taking all of the manuscripts into consideration. The basic thrust of such an interpretation will be
presented in what follows.[22]

Hermeneutics as a "Philological Discipline"

Until now the earliest record of Schleiermacher's
view of hermeneutics was to be found in the first edition
of his so-called theological encyclopedia (1811). In this
work Schleiermacher designates the "art of interpretation"
as a "philological discipline which depends on principles
as firm as those in any other (art)."[23] Schleiermacher,
then, had already conceived of the rules for a properly
artful interpretation as an interconnected whole in opposition to the prevailing view that hermeneutics has to do
only with an "aggregate of observations" that can assist
in the interpretation of particular difficult places.
This initial conception of hermeneutics is described more
fully in the aphorisms "On Hermeneutics" (1805 and 1809,
Ms. 1) and in the "First Draft" (between 1810 and 1819,
Ms. 2). Schleiermacher's actual point of departure is the
assertion--and here he deviated from the generally accepted theological teaching of his day--that the Bible can
claim for itself no special hermeneutical principles and
that it is necessary to construct a general hermeneutics
(Ms. 2, p. 68; Ms. 1, p. 44). This conviction becomes
absolutely fundamental to Schleiermacher, and he teaches
that hermeneutical theory must always be conceived universally and that special applications of its rules can only
occur "by reference to the particular language . . . and
the particular genre" of speech or writing.[24] Hereto-
fore, all hermeneutical reflection on the Bible and the
texts of classical antiquity, with respect to language

and genre as well as contents, time relation, and so
forth, had been confined within given assumptions about
their special normative character (for example, the work
of the theologian Ernesti or the classicists Ast and
Wolf). Schleiermacher contends that these texts should be
understood in the same way as any other spoken or written
expression of a human being. No longer is the problem
merely that of the best or most suitable understanding of
certain definite objects; now understanding itself becomes
problematic. For the first time in the history of hermeneutics Schleiermacher calls attention to the phenomenon
of understanding itself, and he seeks to ascertain its
universal laws (see Ms. 3, pp. 95-97). Thus hermeneutics
acquires a philosophical significance for him, and he becomes more and more aware of this as his thinking develops.

Yet even in the earliest notes, Schleiermacher's
conception of a universal hermeneutics was linked to a
further, questionable view that hermeneutical method
should not be concerned at all with the historical particularity of the item to be understood. The process of understanding is grasped in its universality and is detached
from the special historical conditionedness of the object
it seeks to understand. Indeed, as Schleiermacher himself
says, "one must try to become the immediate reader of a
text in order to understand its allusions, the atmosphere,
and its special field of images" (Ms. 1, p. 43). But to
Schleiermacher's mind this necessary historical knowledge
plays no role in the actual process of understanding. The
appropriation of this knowledge is a subordinate task, the
completion of which is always presupposed in hermeneutics.
Schleiermacher holds to the unexpressed thesis that understanding is a special, self-enclosed process based on its
own universal laws (see Ms. 1, pp. 31-35; Ms. 2, pp. 67-
68). He evidently fails to recognize that knowledge of
the historical context and its gradual appropriation are
integral to the process of understanding itself and that

they can occasionally lead to the decisive step that illuminates the understanding.

In constructing hermeneutical rules, the basic determination of a universal hermeneutics must confine itself to the understanding and not deal with the presentation of that which has been understood. The latter is a second movement that had been included in earlier expositions of hermeneutics. Just as Schleiermacher tried to separate the process of understanding from the appropriation of historical knowledge in order to distill its universal principles, so too he wants to detach the pure conception from the further task of assimilating the thing conceived and to confine hermeneutics to the first. This is the meaning of the first aphorism on hermeneutics, which Schleiermacher formulated in opposition to Ernesti's Institutio Interpretis Novi Testamenti (1st ed. 1761): "Only what Ernesti (Prol., §4) calls subtilitas intelligendi [exactness of understanding] genuinely belongs to hermeneutics. As soon assthe subtilitas explicandi [exactness of explication] becomes more than the outer side of understanding, it becomes part of the art of presentation, and is itself subject to hermeneutics" (Ms. 1, p. 41). In his hermeneutical theory he tried to give expression to what he had already applied practically in the Kritik der bisherigen Sittenlehre (1801): "In the act of judging, one is not in a frame of mind open for a grasp of the content." Rather a pure comprehension must precede any judgment, as something separate from it and existing independently.[25] In the Aphorisms of 1805 there is a corresponding note indicative of historicism: "In interpretation it is essential that one be able to step out of one's own frame of mind into that of the author" (Ms. 1, p. 42). In order to establish understanding as a self-subsisting phenomenon, Schleiermacher was led to dissolve the combination of intelligere and explicare, which even in Ernesti had been only superficial and supplemental. Manifestly, this notion opens up a practice of his-

torical understanding which attempts to leap over historical distances in order to be absorbed in the view of those
who lived in the past. The analogy-structure of all actual understanding, grounded in the fact that one can never
completely free oneself from one's own situation and can
only arrive at something which corresponds to that which
was to be understood, is gradually lost from view.

The decisive, creative aspect of Schleiermacher's
hermeneutics, as expressed in the earlier sketches, espe-
cailly, is the strict and conscious alignment to the concrete process of living speech. In Manuscript 1 we read:
"Language is the only presupposition in hermeneutics, and
everything that is to be found, including the other objective and subjective presuppositions, must be discovered in
language" (Ms. 1, p. 50). In Manuscript 2 we read a similar and even more precise statement: "the work of hermeneutics has to do only with members of sentences" (Ms. 2,
p. 80). Schleiermacher produced his conception of language in opposition to Ernesti's theory that every work
has only one sense [Sinn] (sensus) which unfolds into various meanings [Bedeutungen] (significationes). Schleiermacher taught that every word has a general sphere of
meaning, which "is never found by itself," but is to be
detected only out of the infinite fullness of the applications of the meaning of this particular work (see Ms. 2,
p. 76 and Ms. 1, pp. 42-43, 48, 60, et passim). The general sphere of meaning always eludes thinking, for it can
be grasped and sensed only in its various applications by
"feeling." In Schleiermacher's own words: "Feeling must
be the substitute for the completeness (of the particular
meanings, which is unattainable by considering them suc-
cessively) if the sphere of meaning or the 'essential unity' of a word is to be found" (see Ms. 2, p. 77).

In the hermeneutical process itself the inability of
reason to grasp the essential unity of a word-meaning
leads the interpreter in an apparent circle, as the history of hermeneutics had made explicit by its reference to

understanding the whole from the parts and the parts in
turn from the whole (see Ms. 1, pp. 59, 61-62; Ms. 2,
pp. 68-69). According to Schleiermacher, one can escape
this apparent circle. One must begin by ascertaining the
usage of the given word from the context of the sentence
in which it occurs. Then, by comparing all known applications of the word, one can determine the general sphere in
a provisional way. This provisional grasp of the general
meaning becomes the point of departure for the hermeneutical operations specifically directed toward determining
the special application in each particular case (see Ms.
2, pp. 76-77). The coinherence of universal and particular in every word-meaning which this view presupposes can
be called the individuality of meaning. Understanding
will then consist in construing this coinherence according
to the rules of interpretation. Schleiermacher believes
that a linguistic expression is really understood only
when the individual meaning presented in it is construed
methodically and skillfully. To his mind it does not suffice to apply the hermeneutical rules to those parts of
texts that are particularly difficult. Rather he proposes
the following "maxim": "I do not understand anything that
I cannot perceive and comprehend as necessary" (Ms. 1,
p. 41). In this sense he promotes from the beginning a
"comprehensive treatment" of hermeneutical theory and a
"widening of its sphere" to cover every particular case of
understanding (Ms. 1, pp. 33-37). Furthermore, Schleiermacher asserts: "Every child comes to an understanding of
word meanings only through hermeneutics," which, even
though it is accomplished naturally and unconsciously,
nonetheless ends in a "living reconstruction" (Ms. 1, pp.
48 and 52). The more a person loses this natural, imi-
tating "comparison" of the universal and particular, the
more dependent one becomes on an explicit hermeneutics, if
one's understanding actually deserves to be called by that
term.

In this basic conception of hermeneutics one can see
how the theory of the understanding, which is so closely

oriented to the structure of language and which may be
called a "philological" discipline only in a pretentious
sense, is connected to the stages in the development of
his thought as a whole. In his "Brouillon zur Ethik"
(1805-6) Schleiermacher says that the infinite whole of
the "morally constructed world" is represented in the inner "symbol" of human thinking.[26] It is structured as a
complex coinherence of universal and particular acts of
reason. This inner symbol becomes externally perceptible
in language, and, in correspondence with its individual
structure, the understanding of language consists in reconstructing the unity of universal and particular.
Nevertheless, it seems to be an unsuitable assessment of
the hermeneutical method to say that adults have no immediate understanding in the proper sense of the term, but
must attain it, so to speak, artificially. As a matter of
fact, we always experience actual understanding as a con-
tingent act, and a hermeneutical theory can only be a
guide to it or a support for it.

The particular assertions of Schleiermacher's hermeneutics issue directly from the thought that the task is
to arrive at a general methodological construction
[Konstruieren] of a particular language from the universal
sphere of its words. So-called grammatical interpretation
therefore focuses upon a particular language as a pre-
given fact; it explores the structures of this language
and the fundamental possibilities for expression in it.
It is, therefore, a part of the "construction" of particular applications of meaning from the universal sphere of a
word which is "purely negative and marks out boundaries."
So-called technical interpretation, on the other hand,
seeks to ascertain the individual character of a word
usage "positively," as it is dependent on the power and
mode of speech of a particular person. In the case of a
"use of language" that corresponds completely to its general laws, the two methods would "coincide" (Ms. 1,
p. 42). "(But) the productive spirit always brings forth

something that could not be expected" (Ms. 1, p. 57)! In
each individual expression a person brings about a further
development of the language, which nonetheless remains
bound by the fundamental possibilities of the language.
The language and the person who uses it condition one another. Thus full understanding is attained only as a result of a "repeated oscillation between both" methods of
interpretation, the grammatical and the technical.

Grammatical understanding confines itself to the
"formal" and "material" elements of the language. It
reaches its boundaries at the point where it has to do
with the "tone and accent of the whole" in a given speech
or writing (Ms. 2, p. 88). Then technical interpretation
comes into play. As Schleiermacher puts it: "By a (knowledge of the) individuality (of the author), grammatical
interpretation can be brought to a level it could not have
reached on its own" (Ms. 3', p. 153).[27] In addition to
this "subsidiary use," technical interpretation also has
the task of "grasping the train of thought." But this
task does not require one to inquire behind the language
for a thought somewhere at the basis of what is said. On
the contrary, with reference to this problem Schleiermacher is convinced "that thinking and speaking must be
identical."[28] Thus we also find in Manuscript 3' the
statement: "The maximum extent of this reproduction (of
the train of thought) is imitation--to be able to write on
a given subject in the same way as another would have
treated it" (Ms. 3', p. 154).[29] Technical interpretation
has to do with the "subjective combination" of a particular author, with the distinctiveness of his linguistic
"composition," or--as Schleiermacher can also say--with
his "style" (Ms. 1, p. 56-58). It remains throughout
within the horizon of the given language, and it is emphasized that even "the derivation of the technical meaning"
must conform "to the unity of the word-sphere" (Ms. 1,
p. 50). It aims at finding the "individual use of language," as this individuality presents itself as the unity

of the "universal laws of combination" of a language and
their modification "through the special character" (Ms. 1,
p. 56).

Hermeneutics as a "doctrine of art" [Kunstlehre] or a "technique" [Technik]

The historical development of Schleiermacher's hermeneutics was determined by his desire to set it in relation to the speculative system of his thought which began
to take on a firmer form after 1811. In that attempt he
apparently encountered certain difficulties. In the summary of main principles that he composed in 1819 (Ms. 3),
he tried above all to give a philosophical status to the
"art of understanding." He connects rhetoric or grammar
with his dialectics (doctrine of thinking), which represents the kernel of his philosophy (Ms. 3, pp. 95-98).
But he himself admits that "it is very difficult to assign
hermeneutics to its proper place" (Ms. 3, p. 96), and he
is conscious that his attempt to incorporate it into his
system was only provisional. In 1829 he used for the
first time the expression "doctrine of art" in relation to
hermeneutics. Through this term he hoped to be able "to
present in reputable scientific form the total range and
foundations of the method" (Ms. 5, p. 176). And in the
second edition of the Brief Outline on the Study of Theology (1830) he formulated his concern as follows:

> The full understanding of a discourse or writing
> is an artistic achievement and thus requires a
> doctrine of art or technique, which we designate
> by the term 'hermeneutics.' . . . Such a doc-
> trine of art only exists insofar as its rules
> form a system based directly on clear principles
> drawn from the nature of thinking and language.[30]

As a result of this thinking, Schleiermacher finally
(more than ten years after the first attempt) tried to incorporate his hermeneutical theory into his system of ethics, in the place which he had already, in the sketches on
ethics of 1816, assigned to the doctrines of civic and ed-
ucational art. In that place both doctrines of art serve
as examples of special scientific disciplines which are to

mediate between the essence of humanity or of human society derived from scientific-speculative thought and the
empirical reality that never completely corresponds to the
former. Herein lies a commendable but certainly not adequate attempt to relate philosophical speculation in the
sense of transcendental deduction to experiencable reality, above all to the reality referred to by the positive
sciences. It is presupposed that in the areas of these
scientific disciplines there is a discrepancy between the
ideal inner essence and the empirical external appearance.[31] Applied to hermeneutics, this presupposition results in conceiving the object of hermeneutics as existing
in a twofold manner, as an internal thinking and as an external language modified by empirical givens. With this
conception, Schleiermacher backs off from the thought that
dominated his earlier hermeneutical sketches and that he
could formulate as late as 1813: "thought and expression
are essentially and internally entirely the same."[32] He
no longer asks how the general language is individualized
by the persons who use it or how the symbol of an individually constructed moral world is represented in it.
Rather only inner thinking itself is viewed as such a symbol, which is changed and further individualized in the
external language. More and more the process by which
thinking emerges into empirically graspable linguistic
form becomes the proper object of hermeneutics, with special reference to how in this process of the externaliza-
tion of thinking the individuality of the speaker comes to
be known. The main reason that Schleiermacher waited so
long (1829) before conceiving his theory of understanding
as simply a doctrine of art or technique is that he turned
away only very hesitantly and gradually from the basic
conception, so decisive for this topic, of the identity of
thought and language. Only because of a contradiction in
the subject matter could he surrender the insight that our
thinking as well as our whole being are originally and

essentially determined by the language with which we are given the understanding of our world.

In the introduction to his sketch of 1819 Schleiermacher asserts that thinking and speaking are to be distinguished as ideal and appearance. The aim of hermeneutics, as he designates it there, is "to grasp the thinking that underlies a given statement" (Ms. 3, p. 97). Two primary methods of understanding, each implying and completing the other and corresponding to the modification of thinking through language, must serve this aim. They are the grammatical and the psychological (Ms. 3, p. 99). The task, therefore, is to ascertain how a given thought in this or that author has been changed by its linguistic expression. In order to do this, the interpreter must know the objective condition of the language as it was available to the author, in terms of both its historical development and its possibilities for further development, and he must be informed about the subjective presuppositions of the life and thought of the author under consideration, especially how that life and thought had developed and how it could carry itself forward. Schleiermacher describes "the positive formula" for right understanding as "the historical and divinatory, subjective and objective reconstruction of a given statement" (Ms. 3, p. 111).

Thus is further sharpened the thesis of the early sketches that understanding, when it claims to be exact and adequate, must always be consciously brought about by these methods. "The strict practice," which Schleiermacher wants to establish in his hermeneutics, is based, according to his own words, on the conviction that "misunderstanding occurs as a matter of course, and so understanding must be willed and sought at every point" (Ms. 3, p. 110). The separation of the process of understanding from the knowledge of the historical particularity of a given situation is carried even further in this later conception. This became especially clear when Schleiermacher

began to work out a new theological discipline which he
introduced into his cycle of lectures in 1829. The so-
called "Introduction to the New Testament" should, among
other things, perform the "task" of "placing us (by gathering historical knowledge) in the position of the original readers for whom the New Testament authors wrote."[33]
And research in this discipline should be strictly separated from exegesis and precede it as a preparatory scientific aid.

It is worth noting, however, that Schleiermacher did
not incorporate in the second part of his "Compendium of
1819" those changes which would have been expected from
his statements in the introduction. He did not call the
second part "Psychological Interpretation," as he did in
one of the first theses in the introduction, but "Technical Interpretation," as he had in earlier sketches (Ms. 3,
pp. 99, 147). He explicitly states that one "is to avoid"
everything that can be learned about an author's "distinctive manner of writing" from sources other than his language itself (Ms. 3, p. 149). "The entire aim" of technical interpretation is designated as a "complete understanding of the style" (Ms. 3, p. 148). In agreement with
these statements he states in "The Separate Exposition of
the Second Part" from the time between 1820 and 1829 that
"the individuality of the combination and the presentation" is certainly connected "with every other expression
of the individual." But he firmly holds that "(in hermeneutics) we do not deal with this connection and its mid-
point, but only with the peculiarity of the presentation =
style" (Ms. 4, p. 164). Here it is evident that the total
individuality of the speaker becomes somehow manifest in
the language, but Schleiermacher contends that hermeneutics does not enter into this problem at all. He seeks
instead to show, in connection with his earlier statements
about technical interpretation, that a modification of the
general language takes place through the peculiarity of
the one who uses it. This modification presents itself as

the "individual nature" of the speaker (Ms. 4, pp. 162-64).

Not until the "Academy Addresses of 1829," "On the Concept of Hermeneutics," is the second part of the theory of understanding developed in a way that corresponds to the introduction of 1819 and does justice to the claims of a doctrine of art. Here all hermeneutical methods are put in the service of knowing how to make "the internal process (by which inner thought emerges into external language) so transparent by the divinatory and comparative methods" that "the entire relationship between the production of the thoughts and its formation in language is fully and immediately evident" (Ms. 5, p. 193: The manuscript reads "was full and simultaneous" instead of "is fully and immediately evident," but in my opinion that reading makes no sense.) Schleiermacher sees "each work" as a "part of the author's life, and together with his other acts it forms the totality of his life. Thus it is to be understood only from the totality of the person's acts" (Ms. 5, p. 202). The object of understanding is no longer the given content. It is now the process of movement from the internality of thought to language. Now hermeneutics aims not so much at understanding something as at understanding how something is an empirical modification of an ideal reality.

Schleiermacher developed his last lectures on hermeneutics (Ms. 6, 1832-33) in terms of the position he had taken in the "Academy Addresses." He clearly presupposes that the theory of understanding is a dual complex involving both speculative and empirical aspects, a feature which it has in common with all other technical skills (Ms. 6, p. 215). This conviction leads him to conceive technical interpretation no longer in terms of language as the understanding of a technical (individual) nuance of meaning, but in terms of the psychology of the one who speaks, as a "moment" of one's though structure and its linguistic expression. There emerges an entirely new sec-

tion of the second part of his hermeneutics that deals
with "the order of the composition" or, more exactly, with
the process by which the composition comes into being.
The inner process of thinking must be grasped by the following series of acts: "discover the (seminal) decision,
i.e., the unity and actual direction of the work (psychological); then understand the composition as the objective
realization of that decision; then, [understand] (the)
meditation as (the) genetic realization (both technical).
Then, (discover the) secondary thoughts as (the) on-going
influence of the totality of life (psychological)" (Ms. 6,
p. 223). However, Schleiermacher decided to place only
one major division of hermeneutics alongside grammatical
interpretation, and he called this psychological interpretation. This was subdivided into a psychological task per
se and a technical task, each of which seeks to grasp the
process of "composing" from its own special vantage point.

This final form of Schleiermacher's hermeneutics is
at the basis of the edition of Friedrich Lücke, which in
turn was determinative for its propagation through Dilthey. In this way the substantially convincing and positive thoughts in Schleiermacher's earlier sketches came to
be forgotten. It is the intention of the present edition
to make these thoughts accessible and, if possible, fruitful for current philosophical reflection on the phenomenon
of understanding.

MANUSCRIPT 1

THE APHORISMS OF 1805 AND 1809-10

Introduction

1). Only what Ernesti (Prol., §4) calls subtilitas intelligendi [exactness of understanding] genuinely belongs to hermeneutics.[1] As soon as the subtilitas explicandi [exactness of explication] becomes more than the outer side of understanding, it becomes part of the art of presentation, and is itself subject to hermeneutics. Therefore, by making a special application of the universal rules, hermeneutics may offer suggestions for the proper use of commentaries, but not for writing them.

---

2). In the first part of the subtilitas intelligendi Ernesti correctly analyzes the elements necessary for understanding. That is, he defines the task. The other part deals with solutions and aids for the task.[2]

General Introduction

3). Two divergent maxims for understanding. (1) I am understanding everything until I encounter a contradiction or nonsense. (2) I do not understand anything that I cannot perceive and comprehend [construiren] as necessary.[3] In accordance with this second maxim understanding is an unending task.

Introduction to the First Part

4). The failure to understand particular elements occurs not only in dealing with foreign languages; nor does
it occur simply "because one does not think about anything
but the word." On the contrary, it is due to the fact
that one does not comprehend the entire schematic view
[Anschauung] present in a word-sphere, but is satisfied
with only one of its facets.[4]

_____

5). Division 4 does not agree with 5 unless he treats
it more adequately in the material that follows.[5]

_____

General Introduction

6). Strictly speaking, grammatical interpretation is
the objective side; technical, the subjective. Consequently, grammatical interpretation plays a negative role
in hermeneutical construction, marking the boundaries;
technical interpretation is positive. These two sides of
interpretation cannot always coincide, for that would presuppose both a complete knowledge of and completely correct use of the language. The "art" lies in knowing when
one side should give way to the other.

_____

7). The principles for the use of language and of parallels (Morus, p. 16) are by no means axiomatic but need
to be demonstrated.[6]

_____

8). In interpretation it is essential that one be able
to step out of one's own frame of mind into that of the
author. For example, against Morus, p. 18. Morus completely misinterprets the πᾶν [all] in Romans 14:23, where
he could not remain fast to the strict moral idea but
thought only about the result of the action.[7]

_____

First Part

9). In reality, each word, even a particle, has only
one meaning [Bedeutung], and the various meanings of words
must be understood by tracing them back to their original
unity.[8]

First Part

10). If one regards understanding as the task of hermeneutics and adheres to the insight [Anschauung] that
thought is to be treated neither as something objective
nor as a thing, but as an act [factum], all the false dialectical distinctions among the various senses [Sinnen]
can be avoided.[9]

First Part

11). As Ernesti states, the sense [Sinn] of a word is
simply a more precise determination of its meaning, a special instance drawn from its general sphere.[10]

General Introduction

12). The interpreter must try to become the immediate
reader of a text in order to understand its allusions, its
atmosphere, and its special field of images.

Second Part

13). The classification of texts into works, studies,
and occasional writings is also important for hermeneutics
because it establishes certain relations between the
author and the reader.

Second Part

14). One major difficulty is determining which thoughts
should be regarded merely as signs. For example, amplifi-
cations and hyperboles are only signs of an impression;
sudden insights [Einfälle] are often only signs of a particular state of mind. In short, often the form of a

44

thought is what is being stated, while its substance is merely part of the means of. representation.

Second Part

15). Understanding an author is quite a different matter than the customary way of understanding a writing from its subdivisions.

First Part

16). The ordinary, careless way is to be satisfied with a vague impression of the parts so long as one thinks one has caught the general context.

First Part

17). Barbarisms, especially in the meanings of words, arise from an inadequate knowledge of the range of a word of one's native language and of foreign languages. Example, especially of moral concepts. (δικαιοσύνη, [righteousness], Hellenistic).

First Part

18). How polemics influence the use of insufficiently definite words to which an incorrect secondary meaning is ascribed. For example, mysticism.

General Introduction

19). Introduction. Explanation of Hermeneutics. Narrowing the extent of hermeneutics as Ernesti sees it. Extending its scope. Difficulties which arise from the treatment (for example, ambiguous references) and difficulties which arise from the subject matter. --Division (1) Understanding what the author and the reader have in common. (2) Understanding what is peculiar to the author when the interpreter, as a reader, reconstructs him. (3) Understanding what is distinctive about the reader that leads the author to consider him as someone special and different [Aeusseres].

Second Part

20). The essence of the third part is the true notion of
accomodation. This notion does not apply to all texts,
but only to speeches, occasional writings, and certain
didactical pieces.

Second Part

21). The second part, too, is subdivided into a general
and a special task. The general task is to investigate
the idea, the unity of what has been put together, the individuality of the text. The special task is to investigate the various ways in which the elements are combined,
the psychological and the personal aspects.

General Introduction

22). Language must not fluctuate as a general phenomenon, but must be fixed as a determinate phenomenon between
the general and the specific. --Even aberrations peculiar
to a given era are part of the commonly shared language.

General Introduction

23). The introduction also deals with how the general
principles are related to the Holy Scriptures.

Second Part

24). An author may have meant many words inorganically
and many organically. This is difficult to determine.
Consequently, the sphere of the first must be determined
from the second (Tieck, Schlegel).[11] This includes the
musical aspects, both the tone [ton] and the number, and
the emphases, which arise from the linguistic forms
(οὐρανός, Platonic).

General Introduction

25). The consequences of an exegete's doctrine of inspiration. (Note: Which aspects of hermeneutics are anti-
catholic and which are universally Christian.)

First Part

26). Emphasis, as it was described above, should be sought only in more sophisticated styles; in less sophisticated styles one must assume that it was not used.

_____

First Part

27). The deeper one probes into its elements, the more unexplored the language seems.

_____

First Part

28). An objective view of words leads to a mistaken view of figurative terms. _Facies rosea_, _planto serpens scandens_.[12]

_____

First Part

29). There must be a _similitudo intelligibilis_, and thus all the divine attributes are figurative.[13]

_____

First Part

30). It is mad to ascribe the "true" meaning of a word to a time period prior to the rise of its figurative meaning--white and snow-white.[14]

_____

First Part

31). Also internally, within the meaning of words, much that was originally organic becomes again inorganic with the passage of time, and therefore one must know in which period an author writes. For this very reason, however, one should never ignore the etymology of a word (as Spalding does), lest one assume the inorganic to be eternal and unchanging.[15]

_____

First Part

32). In later periods, combinations are constructed inorganically from simple words which were originally meaningless. E.g., _Befug-niss_.

_____

First Part

33). There is a special basis for even the most common
figurative expressions. For example, nicht über die
Schwelle kommen. Consequently, one must carefully consider the time and the exactness of the usage.

Second Part

34). Some mystical figures of speech, such as light and
knowledge, are by their very nature inexhaustible. In
such cases only the way they have been used can determine
how they are meant.

Second Part

35). To be sure, different styles give rise to different
rules of interpretation, but lex narratio and dogma are
poor distinctions.[16]

First Part

36). History is a strange principle for explaining allegory. Thus even Morus explained the reference to Peter
wrongly [Jn. 21:18-19]. So, too, his explanation of "old
patches" is, to say the least, totally inadequate.[17]

First Part

37). An interpreter who too hastily disregards how a way
of speaking originated is tempted to accuse an author of
being ambiguous, as Heindorf accuses Plato in the cases of
εὖ πράττειν and ὅ τι μαθών.[18]

First and Second Part

38). Emphasis temporaria is not emphasis at all, for it
is not based on the word but is caused merely by a change
in the mood of the author. Compare audivi and urbs in
Morus.[19]

First Part

39). Vir summus without any names given, however, is an
emphasis used to restore to honor a word that has lost its
value.[20]

First Part

40). Even the most common things may be misunderstood.
Kant, for example, did not understand the phrase "most
humble servant," and consequently he did not know a whole
class of words, a whole part of language structure.[21]
Coined words [Scheinwörter] are a sign of modern times.

First Part

41). One cannot understand a language's stage of development without knowing about its entire history and nature, and this is impossible unless one knows the language
as a whole.

General Introduction

42). One cannot understand a spoken statement without
knowing both its most general and its most personal and
particular value.

Second Part

43). Since speaking as such is an elaboration, in speaking something intensive is transformed into something extensive.

General Introduction

44). If every act of speech were a living reconstruction, there would be no need for hermeneutics, but only
for art criticism.

First Part

45). One can observe the various strata of views
[Anschauungen] and ways of viewing in a language. How the
devil sows weeds among the wheat.[22]

First Part

46). On the value of definitions in language. The only
true definitions are those constructed from language's own
combined forms of derivation.

First Part

47). Ellipses are signs of increasing activity. People
no longer have as much time to stop and dwell on things.
Characteristic difference in German between brevity in
common life (many sentences, abbreviated) and business
style (few sentences, complex).

First Part

48). If every spoken statement is viewed with language
as the center, all personal nuance disappears, except in
the case of the true artist of language who individualizes
the language anew.

General Introduction

49). Previous treatments of hermeneutics presuppose an
ordinary level of understanding, an understanding that
does not require art until it encounters something that
does not make sense. Consequently, all of their rules appear arbitrary, special expedients. Moreover, for the
most part they seem inappropriate [schief], because they
refer back to previous errors of interpretation. For example, individual passages are explained in terms of the
aim of the author.[23]

General Introduction

50). The more extensive treatment seems to contain a
contradiction because one first learns to recognize what
is subjective through understanding itself. From this
originates only the demand to hold together opposed statements. This demand holds true for learning a language in
general.
If every spoken statement is understood with the artist as
the center, then everything that is given and available in

the value of the language disappears, except insofar as it grasps the artist and determines his thinking.

---

51). Christianity has created language. From its very beginning it has been a potentiating linguistic spirit, and it still is. It is providential that it could not annex itself to Hellenistic truth.

---

52). Hermeneutics is the reverse of grammar and even more.

---

53). The technical meaning of a term is to be derived from the unity of the word-sphere and from the rules governing the presupposition of this unity. Use of available technical meanings and the rise of new ones.

---

54). Discuss how in judicial hermeneutics meaning is related to the increasing number of cases which are objectively grasped under it. Discuss the difference between exegesis [Auslegen] and eisegesis [Einlegen].

---

55). Language is the only presupposition in hermeneutics, and everything that is to be found, including the other objective and subjective presuppositions, must be discovered in language.

---

56). Words that are precisely and closely determined by sense referents are all technical. For such cases short and simple terms are desirable. For example, the Arabs as hunters and our farmers as cattle-breeders have many words for minor differences between animals, but not for uncultivated ones. (Note: A farmer will just as often subsume colt under draught animal as under horse.)

---

57). Example of how easy it is to understand too little is Schlegel's Poems, p. 189.[24]

---

58). Synechdoche is itself a figure of speech. The connection in the view [Anschauung] is usually presupposed, contento pro continuo, whereas the separation must be explicitly designated. Usually one wants to bring to mind the distinctive view [Anschauung], pars pro toto.[25]

---

59). Just as one must begin with the moral law in order to understand man, so in order to understand a language one must begin with its structural laws.

---

60). Everything complex must be referred back to what is simple; a multiplicity of meanings must be quite consciously reduced to their unity.

---

61). Concerning language usage over against the rules of language. Correct boundary line: respect for linguistic usage.

---

62). So-called synonyms often arise from entirely different views. Hügel [hill] and Berg [mountain, hill], Tal [valley] and Schlucht [ravine, gorge].

---

63). Every concept involves an antithesis. The view [Anschauung] has been absorbed in the inflection. Suchen as an example of how a figurative meaning dissolves into a literal one. Leiter is another example.[26] Profundity of language in the identity of expression for real and ideal view [Anschauung]. One must consider both the theory of synonyms and the theory of the multiple meanings of words in order to come to a correct idea of the nature of a word.[27] In the case of an ambiguous reference, the more grammatical and correct an author is, the more the most natural and most obvious meaning is to be preferred. Often in the New Testament this cannot be determined. ἀπὸ τοῦ καλέσαντος ὑμᾶς ἐν χάριτι Χριστοῦ (Gal. 1:6).

---

64). One quickly understands μετατίθεσθαι άπὸ τοῦ
καλέσαντος, but it is not understood completely until one
has appropriated its entire original meaning.[28]

65). Example of a suddenly separate view [Anschauung] of
a word or of a transfer from one meaning to another.
Galatians 1:10. άνθρώπους πείθω ή τὸν, θεόν.

66). Out of "conferring with flesh and blood" one has
made a "vivid" ["anschauliche"] way of speaking, "going to
court with sensuousness."[29]

67). Figurative meanings are subjective meanings, which,
having emerged from an actual, definite image, have become
objective.

68). Every child comes to understand the meanings of
words only through hermeneutics.

69). The principle of the unity of signification [Sinn]
is the law of grammatical interpretation. At the same
time it is the principle for the definiteness of the meaning, though this meaning follows only from the original
unity of meaning.
(Note: The opposite theory about the multiple meanings of
words is untenable because it confuses the work of technical interpretation with that of grammatical.)

70). It can be said that Paul is the only one who made
use of the treasure of the Greek conjunction, undoubtedly
because he is dialectical.

71). Genetiva consequenti never occur in the genitive
clause of a sentence which conditions another.

72). The ἐν διὰ δυοῖν [hendiadys] comes from making
ideas into substantives. One can speak of figurative

meanings only when there already exists a literal expression for what is indicated.

---

73). When discussing technical meanings, ask whether language becomes more perfect when it becomes more technical. History of the Greek language.

---

74). When raised with respect to God as the author, the question of the infinity of sense [Sinn] belongs to technical interpretation. In mysticism, however, it has a different meaning, which comes to blend [sich verliert] naturally into the investigation of language as a whole.[30]

---

75). Literal and figurative meaning. In tela solis and comae arborum, telum does not mean beam or coma, leaf, for not only the literal meaning but the construction is objective, which serves to eliminate the dead, objective appearance and illuminate the living view [Anschauung]. Therefore, frequently the relationship can be reversed: for example, love and flowers. In other cases there are objects which represent the view κατ' ἐξοχήν. This is the language's power of reproduction.[31]

---

76). By citing one and the same example, Morus refers to syntax as the means for definition (p. 41). Yet on page 46 it is the cause of ambiguity.[32]

---

77). πίστις ᾿αγαθόη in Titus 2:10 is not a Greek usage because the Greek πίστις is in no way fides vox media.[33]

---

78). In the Greek language there are words which refer to both the theoretical and practical spheres, such as δοκει, ἔοικεν, and therefore they signify only degree, as does πίστις. In German this opposition dominates. (Note: Morus' remarks on page 45 about the construction are right.)

---

79). History is a means for interpreting only what is discussed as already having happened, and therefore it is not to be used for the question of fasting (Morus, p. 41; Lk. 5:35), which can be much better understood without history.

---

80). The opinion that a sentence consists of subject, predicate and copula is connected with that of the objective, logical meaning of words, which regards the predicate merely as an abstract entity. The cardinal point of this view is the change of the verb into copula and participle. The question about the copula is never settled unless one assumes an absolute synthesis. In every language the more the copula has been deadened, the more frequently it occurs, especially in verbs.

✓ 81). In order to determine the particular from the universal, one must deal with the formal element first, because that determines how everything coheres.

---

82). There are two kinds of determination, the exclusive, which comes from the whole context, and the thetic, which comes from the immediate context.

✓ 83). The formal element, especially particles, is itself determined by the material element. Conjunctions, for example, may extend parts of the preceeding material or introduce something new.

---

84). The Greeks used special particles to indicate how a discourse was organized. This device is far better than our practice of punctuation.

---

85). The original particles can have either an objective or a subjective meaning. This is one of the limits of technical interpretation.

---

86). One can understand both too little and too much about both the contents and its degree of emphasis [Grad].

---

87). Particles can refer forward to sentences attached to the end or they can refer backward to the beginning.

---

88). The Harris-Wolf theory of Greek verbs is hardly correct. It treats language in an entirely too conceptual and abstract fashion, and gives too little regard to it as living. The theory originally derived from Stoic dialectics. Moreover, it does not completely solve the problem of grammatical understanding. Nor is it completely confirmed by inflection.
The theory of the absolute and conditial which has been applied to modern languages is hardly correct, for the theory must resort to potentiating the verbs by means of helping verbs.[34]

---

89). Many anomalies in the Greek use of modes are derived from the formation of epics in the language. Conditional statements are expressed in the same way as real ones, and so everything proceeds objectively in the indicative.

---

90). Whenever a subject and predicate mutually limit one another in a definite way, there is a phrase [Phrasis].

---

91). When rightly understood, the infinite significance of the Holy Scriptures is not in contradiction to its hermeneutical limitations.

---

92). There are examples in which it seems in a very deceptive way, as if the meanings of a word have gradually increased and expanded. Nonetheless, this impression is still only an illusion.

---

93). The immediate structure as a means of limiting petere aliquem and ab aliquo.[35]

---

94). For the technical limitation one must locate the major passages. But such passages are frequently only incidental in an author's work.

---

95). The extent to which several authors may be viewed as one. Hermeneutical concept of a school. In philosophy, even the changes that develop within a school may serve as parallels for clarification.

---

96). General uses of parallel passages. (1) Secondary determination; (2) adding detail to a general statement; (3) literal expressions explain the figurative ones.[36]

---

97). Especially when dealing with a figurative expression in a parallel area, the interpreter ought not be satisfied with a general resemblance, but go back to the nature of the expression.[37]

---

98). By and large the materials in introductions contain the premises for technical interpretation.

---

99). One must already know a man in order to understand what he says, and yet one first becomes acquainted with him by what he says.

---

100). The general laws of combination, modified by the special character and then by the . . preceding the statement
(Note: Is this modification an expansion or a delimitation?)
Subjective combinations may be either free and arbitrary, as in intimate writings, in occasional writings, or modified by a form, bound, as in artistic writings. However, it would be disastrous to take these distinctions too strictly.

---

101). The statement of the subject matter and the form in
general gives rise to an expectation which is open-ended,
like a schema. The schema which arises is only subjective.

---

102). Expectations arise as soon as the author becomes
too mannered, even when one does not know the subject matter. This is subjective.

---

103). Authors in whose works one finds everything one expects and nothing more are absolutely logical and imper-
sonal.[38] But they are very poor writers. The productive
spirit always brings forth something that could not have
been expected.

---

104). Lyrical poets, who are said to be the most subjective, are the most difficult authors among the ancients to
interpret technically. They speak from epic and gnomic
heights.

---

105). The distinction between free and bound combinations
corresponds to that between common and technical usages of
words.

---

106). The question as to whether the act of combination
is passive or active corresponds to the question as to
whether language signifies concepts or intuitions
[Anschauungen].

---

107). The claim that an author's style is arbitrary corresponds to the usual opinion of how words are used.

---

108). An insistence on expressing one's distinctive character in the same way regardless of differences between
genres is not an internal but an acquired trait. It is
not individuality but a blind personal obstinancy. It is
not style but mannerism.

---

109). Unity is the art of composition, and so it must express itself in a variety of ways according to the variety of genres. It is expressed first in the overall organization of the work. It is finally expressed in the linguistic constructions which help the combination. Note: Instead of the term "combination" it would be better to speak of the "arrangement" of a work. Generally one does not begin with the former consideration, but with the latter one.

---

110). This restriction gives rise to deceptive, groundless observations about individual uses of language.

---

111). When an author rips a passage out of its context in order to imitate a work, it becomes merely an ornament or a mannerism. All such flowery language is the result of the imitator's inability to grasp what is truly individual.

---

112). Even if the interpreter does not recognize the individuality of a work in its overall organization, the organization of the whole is still the basis for the technical interpretation of the various parts because even at this point the general laws of combination are operative.

---

113). On the fact that ancient authors limited themselves to one genre. Founded for the most part in the priesthood and in . . Plato on tragedy and comedy.[39]

---

114). In interpreting the New Testament, as in interpreting all literature, one must consider how in any style the speaker thinks of the combination of thoughts and the way in which the hearers understand. No text is intended in such a way that its hearers could not possibly have understood it. For example, Stange's explanation of Matthew 8: 20. See Jenaische Allgemeine Literatur Zeitung, 1805, no. 183.[40]

---

115). In dealing with historical writings, determining what is pure description and what is mixed with judgments is a matter for technical interpretation, insofar as the author himself is assumed to have been conscious of the difference.[41]

---

116). An author's distinctive use of language must show itself in the modification of the character of the text by which the genre is determined. For any author who is able to give himself entirely to a prescribed form must not be distinctive.

---

117). The ability to say of particular words and ways of speaking, "that is not Platonic or Xenophonic," is usually based more on the linguistic sphere than on the author's distinctiveness.[42]

---

118). Hugo Grotius calls parallel passages <u>coniuncta origine et loco</u>.[43]

---

119). At the beginning of grammatical interpretation, discuss once again the interaction between grammar and hermeneutics. Then, for the first time, add that every individual constructs language; that every understanding of a given text contributes to understanding the language. Consequently, the same principle operates in both.

---

120). The understanding of a given statement [<u>Rede</u>] is always based on something prior, of two sorts--a preliminary knowledge of human beings, a preliminary knowledge of the subject matter. (Note: In the case of a text, either by a study of the author or by a study of the subject matter.)

---

121). The understanding of a particular is always conditioned by an understanding of the whole.

---

122). In order to understand a given topic, one must
start with what is written at the beginning where the special sphere is first identified from what is general.[44]

---

123). This is a general canon for pure historical study.
--Indeed, it is a rule for understanding anything at all.
--How it stands the test in the sphere of common life.
Where this is missing, the first aid. Idea of an intro-
duction to the New Testament.

---

124). The whole is first understood as a genre. --New
genres develop only from larger spheres, and, in the final
analysis, out of life itself.

---

125). The unity of a word is a schema, a displaceable
view [Anschauung].
The first usage of a word is not to be equated with its
meaning.
Just as a word is affected by the twist given by the context, so too is its meaning. One is especially hesitant
to search for the meaning of a word when one wants to attach it to a sense object [sinnliches Ding].

---

126). How to approach indeterminate elements: the less
certain one is of the meaning, the more strictly must one
hold to the given usage.

---

127). In our native language, however, we follow its natural development as the whole as well as in each given
sphere of language. We should proceed in the same way
with foreign languages, relying on a dictionary only to
substitute for the author who is still to be found.
--Further use of a dictionary.
Attention to what is variable [mannigfaltige] is just as
essential as attention to what is determinate.

---

128). The two sides of the whole hermeneutical task must
be separated even before the grammatical operation begins.
Failure to do this leads beginners to make errors. Be
careful in dealing with rare meanings.

---

129). How is meaning determined? First, the material element. Immediate context. Essential components of the
sentence. Contract expanded sentences. Subject and predicate determine each other, and each is determined by its
modifiers. Everything is conditioned by the formal element which must determine how each part fits with the others.

---

130). The subject is delimited both by the whole, insofar
as it is part of the subject matter, and by the predicate,
insofar as it is a secondary representation [Nebenvor-
stellung].

---

131). The two main parts of technical interpretation in-
teract. The more the effort to grasp the thoughts fully
comes to the foreground, the more the direct aids for
grammatical interpretation recede, and vice versa.[45]
--This division always applies. For all aids come from
knowing the train of thought.
(Note: On the significance of the task. Its relation to
grammatical interpretation. Therefore it is a cycle.
The unity may be reduced to style, in the higher sense of
the term.[46] Maximum of knowledge is imitation. Both the
common and distinctive aspects must emerge simultaneously.)

---

132). Investigating the distinctiveness of an author's
style is related to this task in the same way that investigating the unity of words is related to the grammatical
task.

---

133). On the one hand, an author finds himself guided by
the power of the subject matter. This is the objective
side. On the other hand, the author is free. This is the
subjective side.

---

134). A "free" text is generally either popular, when it
is made free for the sake of others, or lyrical, when it
is made free for the author's own sake.

---

135). Just as the first side [grammatical interpretation]
is the reverse of grammar, so the second side [technical
interpretation] is the reverse of composition.

---

136). Just as the unity emerges gradually from the special way words are used, so distinctiveness first emerges
from research into the train of thought.

---

137). Just as elements of the composition carry over the
thoughts into the sphere of expression, so too the elements of expression, the words, cross over into the sphere
of composition. This is true only in that to some extent
in every work a special terminology is formed.

---

138). Friday, March 2.[47]
Knowledge of an author's distinctive treatment of language
emerges from an overview of the work. (1) Material distinctiveness is based on how theoretical the presentation
is. (Note: Distinctive uses of language in other cases
coincide here, but not with the general overview.) (2)
Formal distinctiveness is based on the span between the
objective and subjective elements. A narrow span results
in uniformity, lyrics, epics, Aristotelian. A wider span
results in distance, philosophical, historical.
Often one comes to a false overview. This is a possible
cause for error.
In the case of familiar themes, the interpreter must guard
against a personal bias, for or against.

Friday, March 9.

The object is theoretical, grasping the subjective principle.

Saturday, March 10.

The objective element alone indicates only the material
side of an author's state of mind. With respect to the
train of thought, the objective combination, which must be
conceived as static, is preparatory. Subjective element
by itself. Its connection to the explanation. The first
step is to expand one's idea of the totality of all the
possibilities. (Note: what is actually presented is understood when one understands its objectivity.) (a) Negative side. Caution, prove its necessity. (b) Positive
side. Study the era. --(Our attempts to construct the
individual unity and the train of thought are mutually
conditioning. Therefore, both must be pursued simultaneously. On constructing the individual unity: what is not
present; what requires a special stimulus; what emerges
only under certain conditions which can be easily specified; what emerges only under certain conditions which are
difficult to specify.) --Both attempts are conditioned by
the character of the genre, that is, whether it is strict
or allows latitude, whether it permits much or little subjective leeway. But of course this is to be determined
only by the distance or objective general validity, and
the popular, subjective with a special aim, without a special aim. (Do not confuse these two, even though each
element of the one can just as easily be an element of the
other.) The general, too, has a particular public, but it
is not limited by an transient factor.

Popular elements occur even in works, when the author must
make his public receptive to the new views which he has
discovered.

---

139). Often nothing at all may be concluded from new invented words.

---

140). What is an objective element in one presentation may be subjective in another. Therefore, the material treatment of the subjective element conforms to that of the objective. --This holds particularly for words with somewhat variable meanings. (For what is misunderstood in this belongs to mannerism.)

---

141). Rhythmic "peculiarities," which are difficult to show, are almost always distinctive to an author.

---

142). Saturday, March 17. The linguistic use in a given passage must be found by means of the subjective element. --Much that is taken for this was customary to a time or a class for which we have only a single representative. --One comes to have a feeling for what is distinctive, but it will remain a difficult statement. --Something general in the subjective use of language must correspond to the objective linguistic usage. --A study of rhythm tells us only how the rhythms are related to each other. --Difficulties and violations of rules, wordplays, anacoluthons.

---

143). Friday, March 23.
(1) Combining the objective and subjective so that the interpreter can put himself "inside" the author. (2) On understanding an author better than he understands himself. (a) increasing our understanding, (b) correcting that understanding. (3) On the difference between difficult and easy texts. Objective and subjective causes. (4) The relationship between specialized and general hermeneutics. (a) different relations in both parts, (b) differences between texts, (c) difficulty with the scientific form.[48]

MANUSCRIPT 1'

EXAMPLE OF HERMENEUTICS

144). Plato's Republic, II: 366a. ἀλλ' ὦ φίλε, ψήσει
λογιζόμενος, αἱ τελεταὶ αὖ μέγα δύνανται καὶ οἱ λύσιοι
θεοί, ὡς αἱ μέγισται πόλεις λέγουσι, καὶ οἱ θεῶν παῖδες
ποιηταὶ καὶ προφῆται τῶν θεῶν γενόμενοι οἳ ταῦτα οὕτως
ἔχειν μηνύουσιν.

---

145). That much is created from little produces only
pleasure.[49]

---

146). Plato's Republic, III: 388b. μηδὲ ἄλλα κλαίοντα,
[. . .] ὅσα καὶ οἷα ἐκεῖνος ἐποίησε·
Wolf's misunderstanding: whether the subject changes or
not.
Cf. in the same work, 388e:[50] ὅταν τις ἐφιῇ ἰσχυρῷ γέλωτι,
ἰσχυρὰν καὶ μεταβολὴν ζητεῖ τὸ τοιοῦτον. Example of an
indefinite thought; so too an example of a passage that
cannot be understood without reference to parallels.[51]

MANUSCRIPT 2

THE FIRST DRAFT OF 1809-10

Introduction

1. Starting from the quite limited purpose of interpreting the Holy Scriptures.

    a. Are the books of Holy Scripture as such in a dif-
ferent category than secular books?

One knows that they are holy only by virtue of having
understood them.

Either the first readers believed that the books were
holy and that they themselves were holy, or they considered the books to be altogether human works and so
could understand them only in the usual way.

The customary belief that the Holy Spirit is not to be
subjected to the rules of interpretation is simply erroneous.

The Catholic doctrine of inspired interpretation. But
why do they grant it only to the clergy?

Certainly, one cannot understand the Holy Spirit without the Holy Spirit. But this is a completely different question, and it, too, depends on being interpreted correctly.

    b. Do the Holy Scriptures, by virtue of their special
nature, also require a special hermeneutics?

Yes. But a special hermeneutics can be understood
only in terms of general hermeneutics; otherwise, the
result is still an aggregate. Confusion will always
prevail unless those who are trying to understand have

brought themselves to the level of hermeneutics.

Ernesti.

His work is inadequate. The rules are self-contradictory.[1]

On the necessity of a general hermeneutics.

2. Explanation of hermeneutics.

a. The usual view combines things that do not belong together and therefore includes too much. Presenting what one has understood to others is itself a production, therefore a "text," and so is not hermeneutics, but an object for hermeneutics. This misunderstanding has resulted from the term.[2]

b. On the other hand, the usual view says too little when it limits itself to texts in foreign languages or to passages in a native language that require a kind of translation of their own.

Concerning widespread misunderstanding in every area.

In familiar languages, difficult places arise only because the easy ones were misunderstood.

Specific rules for understanding particular cases always point back to this error.

Two definitions of understanding. Everything is understood when nothing nonsensical remains. Nothing is understood that is not construed. Example.[3]

3. Analysis of the task.

a. It proceeds from two entirely different points: understanding by reference to the language and understanding by reference to the one who speaks.

Because of this double-character of understanding, interpretation is an art. Neither aspect can be completed by itself.

Grammatical and technical understanding. Only in relative terms can the former be called "lower hermeneutics" and the latter "higher."

Forgetting the author in grammatical interpretation and the language in technical. Taken to its extremes. Praise of speech as a language-forming spirit.

b. Discuss the relationship between grammatical and
technical interpretation. There may be a minimum of
grammatical with a maximum of technical and, vice versa, a minimum of technical with a maximum of grammatical. Numerous variations between these two extremes.
The more objective the statement, the more grammatical; the more subjective, the more technical.

On combining grammatical and technical interpretation.
Since each operation presupposes the other, they must
be directly combined. This is necessary even when one
occurs only minimally, because I do not know this is
the case in advance.

Grammatical interpretation is chiefly concerned with
the elements which characterize the central subject
matter. Technical interpretation is chiefly concerned
with the over-all coherence and with its relation to
the universal laws for combining thoughts. At the
very beginning, therefore, one must immediately grasp
the over-all coherence. The only way to do this is by
quickly reading over the whole text.

Relationship to Philology. It is the reverse of grammar. It is the reverse of composition. Not better
than the two.

c. Indirect analysis of misunderstanding. Qualitative. False part of an entire sphere--can result from
both operations, grammatical and technical.

Quantitative misunderstanding. Understanding too little. Understanding too much is also twofold.

Every error is productive.

One must understand as well as and better than the
author.[4]

4. Arrangement

The two operations are combined in the actual application. In dealing with the rules, however, the two
must be separated because each has its own special
focus.

The main divisions are, first, grammatical interpretation and, then, technical. Grammatical interpretation comes first because in the final analysis both what is presupposed and what is to be discovered is language. Each operation is to be carried out as far as possible, but we will also point out the natural points of connection that lead from one to the other.

The goal of each operation is to avoid qualitative and quantitative misunderstandings.

Grammatical Interpretation

It is the art of finding the precise sense [Sinn] of a given statement from its language and with the help of its language.

The first canon is: one should construe the meaning from the total pre-given value of language and the heritage common to the author and his reader, for only by reference to this is interpretation possible.

In this canon, then, language seems to be divisible. And it is. No one possesses it in its entirety. Language may be divided in terms of time and space: in temporal terms, through growth, i.e., appropriation of foreign elements, through internal combinations and distinctions, and through alliteration; in spatial terms, through provincialisms and dialects.

Provisional application to the language of the New Testament. Its idiom comes from the boundaries of two languages and two ages.

This canon pertains to both qualitative and quantitative misunderstanding, for the richness of meaning depends on when and where a work arose.

One can go into greater detail only by applying this rule to the individual parts, that is, to the words and constructions.

This is the most important and comprehensive rule because every effort to determine and fix the meaning of particular passages by interpreting them separately should be

part of a cumulative process that ultimately determines
the precise meaning of any particular passage in terms of
its context.   But this result is possible only if the various usages of a given element are mutually related in a
way that parallels the changes of the language in general,
that is, if all of the particular meanings can be grasped
under a common schema, as all the variations and altera-
tions of a language display a certain character.   This ap-
lies to both the formal and material elements of language.

This contradicts the customary view of the plurality of
meanings according to which in many cases the original
meaning is regarded as only a distant occasion for the
other meanings.

The invalidity of this customary view becomes clear when
the two opposing theories--that of the manifold meanings
of one word and that of the nearly identical meaning of
totally different words--are combined.   By making this
combination one can see that the entire formation of the
language would be highly "distorted."[5]

Thus it is evident that this customary view puts together
what language keeps apart and vice versa, and, therefore,
that it proceeds from an entirely different standpoint.

In short, this judgment proceeds from the standpoint of
the logic of the concept, whereas language, in its formation, is related to an intuition [Anschauung]: the range   /
of every word is determined by an intuition.

Names of organic concepts, verbs, and adjectives which all
proceed from one schema.

This accounts not only for the multiple meanings of a
word, in that the variety of ways in which this intuition
reoccurs can be subsumed under quite different concepts,
but also for the synonymy of words, in that the relationship can be reversed.

This also accounts for the individuality of languages
since the intuitions may be determined according to very

different points of view [Gesichtspunkte], and what is construed from these different viewpoints can no longer be harmonized. Concepts, however, must be brought into pure relation to one another. Therefore, as a rule, in primitive languages [Ursprachen] no word in one corresponds completely to a single word in another.

This point of view is useful in gaining a clear understanding of so-called "multiple meanings." --Specify these according to the customary antitheses. By relating these to their founding intuitions they may be reduced to the following.

1. That a particular instance, because it is the customary one, is viewed as constituting the entire range of the original meaning. For example, this is frequently the case with metaphors and always the case with metagony. For example:

a. Terms can refer to both movement and form when the movement designates the genesis of the form. planta, serpens.[6]

b. Terms referring to the theoretical and practical realms are often identical (e.g., δοκεῖν, ἔοικα) because knowing is intuited also as an activity.

c. This also applies to the ideal and the real. Many sense-oriented expressions, e.g., over and under, bright and dark, bear clear indications that they are not purely oriented to the senses, as one term of antithesis is taken positively and the other negatively. This indicates that a general intuition governs them. Thus, in nearly every language we find light and darkness used to refer to the intelligible, both in its theoretical and practical aspects.

2. That the content of the intuition is delimited to a particular by a sphere already given by the context. This includes:

a. Those aspects of the act of speaking governed by the formula continuo pro contento. The sphere within

which the <u>continuo</u> is connected with the <u>contento</u> is
already given, and the whole is regarded as an el-
lipse, such that what is presupposed as known in the
particular is already present in the whole.
b. All technical terms, especially, whether scientific, religious, political, or demiurgical. In the latter category the origin of many words, e.g., names of
instruments or even of transactions, is difficult to
explain, for the most part because they arise from un-
cultured peoples. This is true for the terminology
used in games. --In the case of scientific matters we
should note that they are treated in large measure by
means of concepts, and so, for the sake of brevity,
each concept is represented by a specific word. Consequently, the generalization, which applies to every
sphere that is made into an explicit object of study,
that one expects greater precision in its distinctions
and wants to know how it happens that similar matters
are treated as opposites, is modified here so that one
regards the context as subsumed in an inclusive intuition and expects to determine the meaning of words by
definitions.

————————————

There also arises a pretension that scientific expressions should be "exact," but this pretension can never
be fulfilled. There are always terms that are commonly called "figurative," and even when that does not
seem to be so, it is only because the terms are no
longer grasped genetically. This is an "ossification"
and therefore a ruination of language, and the only
possible remedy for it rests with what science is able
to see by constantly renewing itself from the very
center of its intuition and with the rejuvenated and
living terminology created by this renewal. --If
philosophy is the center of all science and if philosophy itself is based on intuitions of a higher order,
then one can see that the hegemony of the concept is

only a point of transition for language. The notion
that the true perfection of language is reached when
it becomes figurative goes together with the notion
that the concept is the highest element in science.
3. That one confuses something belonging to technical interpretation with something belonging to grammatical. Included here are most metaphors, representing a kind of extension of meaning, such as coma arborum, tela solis,
where the words retain their literal meaning and the author relies on a combination of ideas to make the words
exercise their effects.[7] Technical allusions develop in
this way: word plays, the use of proverbs, allegory, where
grammatical interpretation is entirely appropriate and the
question about the author's actual meaning belongs to
technical interpretation. The most common example here is
when the thought itself, as explained by grammatical interpretation, is not part of what is represented, but only
part of the representation, itself a sign. Where and how
this occurs can be discovered only by technical interpretation.

On whether the principle of the unity of meaning applies
to the formal element, the structure. At first glance it
seems unlikely simply because the two are opposites: words
always signify something objective and fixed, whereas the
structure is merely a relation among ever-changing elements. It seems unlikely, too, because the structures of
every language almost always mesh with homogenous elements in other languages.
This assumption must be changed when one observes the following.
1. That the opposition between the material and formal elements is mediated by formal words or particles
which, though signifying only relations, have the
character of independent words, and are subject to
their law.

2. That what is signified only by particles in some languages can be signified only by structure in others, and vice versa. In many languages both particles and structure can be used, and this points to an identity. Therefore, it is an essential part of the individual characteristic of various languages that one will have few particles but many modes of inflection (e.g., Hebrew) while another will have many particles and few modes of inflection (e.g., German) and a third will have a large number of both.

3. Particles are not the only such connectives that can be replaced by the structure, for a large number of pronouns and adjectives can be as well. (Note: Here, as in cases where both occur, the elements are not to be assumed synonymous, though with respect to the presupposed opposition there is a similarity. It is incorrect to regard the suffixes in the Hebrew language as pronouns and the prefixes as particles. They are only modes of inflection. Elements from which other languages would make pronouns and adjectives are in Hebrew built onto the word for a given case. They are permanent only in the sense that they are a type of linguistic construction, and it is just that which is characteristic of structure. In other languages inseparable particles represent a median-point between these two forms.) In reality, then, the opposition already seems to have been eliminated.

4. Were one to consider the question more closely and to recall what was stated about the meaning of words, that is, that material elements do not grasp their so-called objects as fixed and objective but as living and developing and that for this reason many material elements only express relationships, one would see the following. There does exist in language and its sphere an opposition between what is eternal and what is transient, but this opposition does not pertain to the individual elements of an actual language (and the

words "God" and "eternal" can hardly be exempted), for in these elements both are unified with [a] relative difference.

It may be concluded, then, that the principle of the unity of meaning holds for the formal element no less than for the material. Every particle and every inflection has its own basic meaning. Each usage is related to this basic meaning as a particular to the general, and each usage relates to another usage as one particular to another.

Therefore, each usage is a particular in which the essential unity is mixed with an accidental element. The essential unity, then, never emerges as such. Thus in a given case the interpreter cannot determine one particular from another or one usage from another because an intuition is already contained in it. Rather, an unknown usage can be determined only with the aid of the essential unity. But this essential unity is never found as such. Therefore, knowing the essential unity of a word is not a presupposition for determining a given usage, but the unity is to be sought. Consequently, the task of grammatical interpretation is divided into two parts: (1) the task of determing the essential meaning from a given usage and (2) the task of ascertaining an unknown usage from the meaning.

How does one get hold of the meaning? That is, how does one first arrive at a given usage and then go farther? How does one learn to understand in the first place? It is the most difficult operation and the foundation for all others--and we accomplish it in childhood.

For a child every instance of relating a name to an object must seem indefinite. It does not become definite until after many comparisons, and comparison demands reference to particulars. Only by means of associating and comparing particular meanings does one begin to grasp the inner unity. The inner unity is that which is representable in every particular instance of the intuition. But since the completeness of the particular is never reached, the task is unending. Is there any substitute for this completeness? And even if one had such a substitute, would there be any guarantee that one had grasped the inner unity accurately? The guarantee could not be another rule having to do with method. It could only be feeling. Thus this feeling must be the substitute for completeness.

The foundation for the certainty of this feeling must be that every given usage may be easily coordinated to the presumed unity and that this coordination is appropriate to the character of the language. But this is confirmed only by analogy with several other unities, and it therefore becomes certain only along with others. Grasping the character of a language by means of the reflection of the totality of thinking in that language is possible only in the case of primitive peoples living close to nature.

Others can do it only by comparing several languages. One who has lost his philological innocence must for the most common cases rely on philological science.

The task can be completed only by approximation.

Since it is difficult for an individual person to penetrate to the unity of words, it must also be difficult for people as a whole. Thus it follows that any fully developed language passes through three stages: (1) that in which there is not yet a clear consciousness of the unity of its words; (2) that in which this consciousness has extended to the entire language; and (3) that in which this richness in turn leads to confusions and false applications. However, even the unity of words is itself historical and develops. And this holds for the provisional application of the rule which I have stated. To derive a given usage, one must proceed from that clarity and determinacy of the unity of words which could be common to the author and the original reader.

———————————

Dictionaries serve as substitutes for the richness of a given analogy of the particular either generally or momentarily. Therefore, they can be put together from only one of two viewpoints.

    1. Either the unity is posited as unknown: then they are only compilations of discrete usages with references which allow one to verify their correctness. The commentaries of Buddaeus are models of this type.[8]

    2. Or they presume to have discovered the unity of the words: they then present the individual usages as proof. But instead of the true unity, which never actually appears and for which therefore there are no examples, they focus on a particular usage, either the most common or the most tangible as the so-called most proper meaning and make deductions from this. This is an error, and the first rule is to use this type of dictionary as if it were one of the first type, and to deny provisionally every judgment it makes.

A dictionary put together from the second point of view must have a mastery of the spirit of its language, and, were it to specify the unity of the words, it would have to include all of the data for a systematic presentation of the peculiar type of intuition inherent in that language. But the more successful it is in this respect, the less inclined it would be to explain one language by reference to another, that is, to identify word-spheres in two different languages. Instead, it would tend either to confine itself to its own language or to make comparisons with a full awareness of the differences between the languages, and always only in individual cases. A thoroughgoing comparison with a language and its derivatives works only when the one is a close relation or an original source. Nonetheless, most dictionaries make such one-sided comparisons because they never regard the study of language as a goal in itself, but merely as a means. Thus the second rule is that in dealing with original languages one should deny all identifications of word-spheres from the outset.

Once one has a number of clear and distinct usages by collecting analogies or by referring to dictionaries, the rule for discovering the unity is to put together the contrasting meanings. The more completely these contrasting meanings are resolved into a single meaning which underlies all of them, the more certain it is that one has discovered the underlying unity.

(Moreover, in this process the schemes found in dictionaries are not to be used until after the general errors which I mentioned above have been corrected. At best, out of these schemes, but at any rate by means of comparing the most radically opposed formal elements, the way of viewing the world [Anschauungsweise] peculiar to a given people must emerge.)

Certain cautions in this procedure are self-evident from what has already been said. Above all, one must not fail to distinguish the various stages of the language's development. One ought not, however, to look for stages in purely temporal sequence because during the flowering and highest life of a language they all coexist.

From what has been said above it follows that this procedure also applies to the search for the unity of the formal elements.

Here too one must treat each language individually and not try to equate the elements of different languages. Grammarians commit the same mistakes as the lexicographers, with both particles and inflection.

Detailed explanation, by citing various examples and by applying the rules set forth above to the formal element in its entirety.

To be sure, if one starts from the absolute difference among languages, a comparison of languages can be an important means of finding the way of viewing the world. [Anschauungsweise], namely, the way of grasping relationships, peculiar to each.

The main task of grammatical knowledge is, presupposing a knowledge of the meaning of every given case, to find the actual usage which the author had in mind, avoiding not only false meanings, but an overestimate or an insufficient grasp of the meaning as well.

Recall the basic principle of the relationship of various particular usages to their unity. That is, a particular usage is not an expansion or a derivation but a delimitation of the entire sphere.

From this follows the general rule for grammatical interpretation: this delimitation is determined in each case by the context.

The work of hermeneutics has to do only with members of sentences. Every sentence consists of material and formal elements. Therefore, each element is the condition for understanding the other. Consequently, this task, too, is indeterminate and can be resolved only by approximation.

1. Discovering the particular usage of the formal element.

a. Determinability of the formal element by the material element. The material element is of special help in specifying which elements are connected by determining whether a subordinate statement is part of the given train of thought or introduces a new topic. In this way the material element helps to prevent assigning too much or too little meaning because of the identity or difference of the subjects or predicates in different statements. (Note: The nature of the formal element is originally determined by the explicit or implicit character of the type of treatment-- epic, historical, philosophical, familiar, lyrical.)

b. Determinability of the formal element by its two opposing components. Specifically, particles and inflection often jointly construct a whole which, because of this construction, is a more delimited whole. Moreover, the opposition between particles and inflection is modified by the use of the particles.

General reservations about both a and b. One cannot
expect to determine the usage of the formal element
solely by reference to what has preceded. One must
also take into consideration the further development.
Demonstration of this point with reference to a and b,
especially a.

Difficulties in the task, starting with secondary difficulties in dealing with free structure. It is often
difficult to determine which formal elements belong
together, or which formal elements belong to which material elements, or how the material elements are related to each other. These problems are intensified
by homonyms of grammar or by improperly relating inflection and particles. Here one must consider along
with everything else a lack of mastery of the language, which is always to a greater or lesser extent
related to the peculiarities of the language.

Incidental remark about the value of connected and
free structures. The former cannot possibly fructify
a language and make it a living entity. At the very
least such a language is deaf and dumb--an epithet, by
the way, which is applicable quite literally to the
French language. Thus such a language can be only a
tool, and indeed, only a tool of personality. Both
its mode of forming concepts and its constant protru-
sion of personality make the French language a model
of corruption. The desire for a universal language is
a madness which arises naturally from these two rules.
Main difficulty. The more comprehensive the unity,
the more difficult it is to grasp the concrete individual usage. When the unity is so comprehensive that
it is vague and unbounded, one cannot expect to reach
a more definite understanding of the nature of the
language than that which the speaker himself could
have given. Modern languages tend to multiply as well
as to freeze unities. But this problem frequently occurs in dealing with ancient languages too.

Application to the New Testament. (1) Throughout, the
authors have an unclear consciousness of the language.
This fact must always be taken into account. (2)
Since its unity is a mixture of general images from
Greek and Hebrew, it is often doubtful which source
determined a given usage. Consequently, there are often different, equally probable explanations. (3)
Moreover, the original mode of determination is often
lost. For example, the external character of poetry
in Hebrew is lost in Greek. Parables. Sentences.
Difficulty of determining the meaning of time particles in the historical writings.

2. Discovering the definite use of the material element.
a. Determinability by the formal element. The linguistic structure helps indicate the particular delimitation. The nouns and verbs are constructed by use
of various prepositions and cases. Note: This is not
as important as it is commonly believed, not completely different meanings (for example, petere
aliquem and ab aliquo), but light is always shed on
which element of the total intuition [Anschauung]
predominates or recedes.[9]
Consequently, this consideration helps above all to
prevent qualitative misunderstandings, and it is more
useful for dealing with the immediate context than
with the whole.
Application to the New Testament. Here the consideration of the formal element is less helpful and must be
used with greater caution because of the way the authors made "passing" use [momentanen Gebrauch] of formal elements.
b. Determinability by the material context. This applies to both the whole and the particular.
1. Application to the whole. The subject matter
and the pre-established form of treatment determine the relationship between the primary and secondary themes of the work, and by reference to

these two factors one can determine the relationship.

2. In dealing with any given material element, the main rule holds: the subject must be
clarified by the predicate and the predicate by
the subject. Note: (1) When each delimits the
other in a particular way there arises what is
called a _Phrasis_. (2) Clarifications made by reference to the other parts of speech are included
here, since these can be traced back to the simple sentence comprised of subject and copula.
(3) Determining the meaning by reference to the
over-all context tends to exclude various alterna-
tives; that by reference to the immediate context
provides a more positive result.

Other aids.[10]

1. If the subject cannot be determined directly
by the predicate, then it can be determined mediately by the "predicate" of its antithesis. But
one must be certain of having a true antithesis.
One should prefer those antitheses found in the
immediate context over those found farther away.
The ancient languages placed the antitheses in the
immediate context and indicated them even more
clearly by the language itself. Note: Such antitheses can always be found in highly coherent passages, for nothing can be treated coherently without antitheses. But it is difficult to be aware
of the exact calculus of the antitheses and of the
constant, selfsame view of the author. Preliminary readings of the whole are necessary in order
to recognize its arrangement and to know whether
and where help of this sort may be expected.
Application to the New Testament. Due to the peculiar nature of composition in Hebrew there are
many direct antitheses. But little help can be
gained from the more distant antitheses because

the authors wrote so imprecisely. Moreover, the
major antitheses--spirit and flesh, . . and . . ,
light and darkness, heaven and earth--are so vast
and all-encompassing that they may be determined
in many different ways.

2. If a word cannot be explained by the context
in which it appears, then it can be explained from
other contexts or from parallel passages in which
it appears.[11]

Condition for applying this rule. There is never
a "living" or precise identity. Consequently, a
second passage is to be used only when it is certain that the material element is being used in
the same way in both passages. But how can this
be known since the usage in the first passage is
unknown? (1) Parallel passages in a single, coherent text. They are either "near" or "distant."
This distinction is not based on their location in
the text, but on the way the text is organized. A
passages is "near" when it lies in an unbroken
thought sequence with the material which preceded
it. A passage is "distant" when it lies in a section of the work that is not in continuity with
the material that preceded it. (Note: Passages
which are separated only by a transitional sentence may also be regarded as "near." Here, too,
an overall view of the whole is necessary.) The
more strictly scientific the text, the easier it
is to distinguish the "near" and the "distant."
It is natural that (a) A word used as a subject in
a developing sequence of thoughts is used in the
same way throughout. Expressions similar to wordplays are exceptions to this statement. In such
cases, however, the antithesis which helps determine the meaning is expressly indicated. (b) A
word used as a predicate is used with the same determination whenever it is bound together with a

given subject. Here, however, the identity of the subject is more an identity of its sphere in relation to the subject matter of the text. "Distant" passages lie outside of the context which contains the passages to be explained. Thus attention should be directed to the identity of the thought or sequence of thought, and to the relationship between the expression to be explained and the thought. The more scientific the text, the easier it is to decide. The freer the text, the more the decision about parallelism is based on an aggregate of particular, quite unrelated instances.

Extending the applicability. Once the interpreter goes beyond the immediate context, then, by complying with this rule, he need not restrict himself to a single text or to the same author. But he must not go beyond the limits established by these rules.

Thus an author who has written in more than one genre is to be regarded as a different author in each case, except with respect to his unique use of language.

Conversely, a group of authors who belong to the same sphere, period, or school are to be regarded as a single author and used to explain each other. Note that (1) this leads back again to the rule that in grammatical interpretation a speaker is regarded entirely as the organ of language, and that (2) information can also be gained from various schools from the same period and from various periods of a given school in order to identify the common element amid the differences. But this, naturally, belongs to a higher understanding of which the author himself was unaware.

How are parallel passages to be used? (1) The
more technical the language, the more helpful they
are (a) because in such cases several passages can
be used, and (b) because in such cases certain
passages near the beginning give orderly definitions. (2) The more careless and non-technical
the language, the more difficult it is to use parallel passages. Application to the New Testament.
It is especially difficult. To be sure, all of
the books form a single whole, as the product of
one idea and as the school of one master. At the
same time, however, the language is not technical.
Rather the authors strove to create a technical
language from an ancient language that was inadequate to convey the ideas and from a language of
the common people.

Parallel passages can provide assistance in the
following ways: (1) they provide an example that
may help to determine the sphere of a common expression, or (2) they provide a secondary determination that indicates the boundaries of the
sphere, or (3) they provide a sentence which repeats the same contents in different words, or (4)
they provide a one-sided expression that may help
to explain a part of an expression that was not
understood because its antithesis could not be
specified. Note: One ought not simply equate
them, but also seek the basis for their difference.[11]

The preceding discussion applies more to reducing
qualitative misunderstanding. We must speak further about

[3]. Discovering the proper determination of the quantity
of meaning, so that one never seeks too much or too little.[12] Note: (1) Works on hermeneutics usually treat this
topic under the heading of emphasis, but it encompasses a

good deal more than that. (2) Here too one must distinguish between understanding an author al pari and that by
which one sees beyond him.

The various degrees of meaning depend on the language's
stage of development. In the first period a sufficient
number of differences has not yet been found. Consequently, the duplicity of expression which is the basis for
higher meaningfulness is not yet present. In the second
period the differences have been discovered, but the use
of the original unity has not yet been lost. Here, therefore, there can arise a clear awareness of the different
operations and their grounds. In the third period all of
the antitheses have been formed, but the original identity
in the language has been lost. Here, then, expressions
which stem from that identity are regarded as idle affec-
tations and used as such.

Causes of falsely interpreting meaning in the New Testament. (1) Like other ancient texts (Moses and Homer) it
is taken to be the source of all wisdom. Thus, contrived
interpretations have arisen, and there is an unwillingness
to entertain the possibility that it could contain anything insignificant. (2) In accordance with the theory of
verbal inspiration people have (a) assumed an infinity of
meanings in the text and (b) followed the maxim that expressions are to be regarded as figurative only when there
is no other possibility.[13]

With respect to the religious sphere, the New Testament
actually stood in the first period of language-develop-
ment. The antitheses, even those against Judaism, had not
yet been fully developed. One perceives throughout a
striving against the language so that even in the identity
of expressions the difference of the signified objects
could be indicated. To be sure, this was followed very
quickly by the third period, after a passage through the
second which in part occurs in the New Testament itself.
But the third period cannot be found anywhere in the New

Testament, and the interpreter must place himself firmly
within the second.

It is difficult to give general rules for determining the
correct meaning. The context provides the accent and the
tone of the whole, but the interpretation will go wrong if
one seeks to derive too much or too little from them.

Appendix

1. Concerning misconceived maxims of interpretation which
are not permissible in a coherent procedure.

    a. Similarity to history, experience, sound under-
standing. Someone could relate a story falsely.
There is no judge over experience just as there is
none over sound understanding.[14]

    b. Similarity to doctrine, therefore to the task of
resolving contradictions. These two must be kept separate from one another. That was done in the lectures, for the two were treated in different lecture
periods.[15] These lectures also deal with an extension, based on parallels, that several authors can be
regarded as one.[16] But such an application is incorrect, for the extension can relate only to linguistic
meaning. Deviations in teaching can occur in any
school, because each member makes various modifications.

Concerning how to resolve contradictions.[17]

    1. Dogmatic contradictions. --If a contradiction is
only apparent and therefore is based on an erroneous
interpretation, then the error should lead us to notice others. If there really is a contradiction, then
elaborating and expounding the interpretation is of no
benefit, because the more artificial the interpretation, the more surely false it is. Except in a critical sense, then, a contradiction is not even a clue,
and other difficulties will have to be found in the
interpretation. Even a self-contradiction of an author is to be regarded in this way, provided that the

contradictory elements do not come from the same moment. Everyone must have the right to change his
mind.

2. Historical contradictions. Occur among eye-wit-
nesses, especially. It is natural for people to recount events differently. In relating several similar
events, as opposed, for example, to anecdotes, it is
natural not to confuse them. It is also natural for a
person to tell the same incident differently, depend-
ing on his mood, his audience, and his purpose.

Application to the New Testament

With respect to doctrine the New Testament authors are
to be viewed as a school. Most of the contradictions
are only apparent, due to a lack of precise definition. Paul and James gave different meanings to
πίστις [faith]. With respect to the historical materials the notion of inspiration has been overempha-
sized. A story is never complete; if it were it would
stretch out to infinity. Even if the authors were
only instruments of the Holy Spirit, there would still
have to be differences among them. The construction
of "harmonies" is not the business of hermeneutics but
of historical criticism. But criticism can aid technical interpretation.[18]

3. Concerning the use of interpretations offered by others.

a. A commentator or scholiast offers only one opinion, and that opinion must be proven hermeneutically.
Used properly, commentaries serve only to direct attention to matters that otherwise would have been
overlooked.

b. Those who write glosses can serve as effective
witnesses only to the extent that they have either
lived in the identity of the linguistic usage--which
is not the case with either the secular or New Testament glossators--or, as is readily clear, provided
valuable parallel passages.

4. Concerning the use of commentaries in grammatical interpretation. Apology for having omitted examples which in practice would have had to be connected to the other operation, but the data for evaluation was never at hand. Thus, it can be concluded that only an elementary use of commentaries is proper. Lexicographical and grammatical. All reading and even daily life provide occasions for such use.

MANUSCRIPT 2'

A LOOSE PAGE FROM 1810-11

The task. To discover the distinctive character of the
composition from the idea of the work.
Explanation.
 1. The author's "choice" refers to the relation between the possibilities of combination open to him and
 his actual application of them.
 2. Digressions, accessory works, details indicate the
 author's attitude [Gesinnung].
 Here, especially, (a) the strictness of style--this
 often seems to be a trait common to works with a given
 content; (b) the popularity--this is regarded as a
 trait of the genre. But this is an elementary consideration. Of course, one must consider the subject
 matter. The difference between major works and occasional writings.
Condition. One must know all the possibilities that were
at the author's disposal.[19] --Tools for grasping this are
analogy, writers of a similar sort, antithesis. --Great
care on account of the era.
It could be said that this individuality must be immediately apprehended. This is the other antithesis. Both
are to be applied in various cases and in various degrees.
Application to the New Testament.

The distinctive use of language.
Introduction.
1. The more distant and simple the language, the greater the latitude.
2. The range extends from the given usage to its place in the linguistic system.
3. There are two tasks.
First task. Determining the linguistic sphere of the author:
1. By reference to the character of the text, historically, philologically. By itself this consideration does not get at the distinctive use of language.
2. By reference to the character of the age. This consideration works in a restricting manner. Many belong more to the present and to the future than they can show by the language.
3. By reference to the prevailing prejudices and views about the language, both as these govern, yet can describe, the distinctive use of language and as they are used as a means of representation.
Means for determining the linguistic sphere.
1. From theory--and universal rules which, however, are not able to grasp the individual aspect at all.
2. By comparing the material given in one sphere with its opposite. Xenophon, Theophrastus, Plato.
Corollary. It is difficult to apply this technique to traits which appear only once, as in Pindar, and, in many respects, Plato.
The components of a linguistic sphere:
1. Selection--words pass away, words are excluded [ausgeschlossen];
2. Usage--the same situation prevails.
Application to the New Testament.

Second task. Determining the distinctive use of language from the linguistic sphere.
Explanation. It is true subjectivity. The individuality of one author can extend throughout several lin-

guistic spheres; in different authors the individuality may be found in the same . . [sphere].
Twofold method. Immediate intuition and comparison.
Each must aid the other. Comparison alone never
reaches individuality. Immediate intuition can never
be communicated. The two are mediated by a comparison
with the totality of the linguistic sphere.
The main steps. 1. The author's choice of the elements, words, meanings of words, formal elements or
structure. 2. Arranging the particulars into a whole
according to his freedom with the language.

1). When grammatical interpretation can go no farther.[20] a). ἅπαξ λεγόμενα [expressions with only one
known occurrence] or similar cases. 1). When the
parts of a sequence of though which are closest together belong together. Everything standing between
them . . ; compare hyperboles with . .
2). When they do not belong together. a). Refer to
the material that leads up to the passage. Ask with
what the complex can close. b). Refer to the material that follows the passage. Ask how this author
would "project" his thought. Note: Not merely in logical terms, but in terms of his individuality.
b). Figurative expressions [Tropos]. 1). Not figurative, and ordinarily determined by the context.

1. On the logical coherence. 2. Parallels to similar passages. 3. In the end, after "repeated"
readings, the extremes come together. With respect to
this problem, both the power of the language and the
power of the idea merge.

MANUSCRIPT 3

HERMENEUTICS: THE COMPENDIUM OF 1819

AND THE MARGINAL NOTES OF 1828

Begun on April 19, 1819 with four lectures per week

Introduction

I. 1. At present there is no general hermeneutics as the
art of understanding but only a variety of specialized
hermeneutics.* Ast's explanation, p. 172; Wolf, p. 37.[1]

---

*1828

1. Hermeneutics and criticism are related such that the
practice of either one presupposes the other.
In both, the relationship to the author is general and
varied.
Hermeneutics is presumed to be unimportant because it is
necessary where criticism is hardly applicable at all, in
general because the task of criticism supposedly ends,
whereas the task of hermeneutics is endless. The hermeneutical task moves constantly. My first sentence refers
to this movement.
2. With respect to its study of both genre and language,
special hermeneutics is only an aggregate of observations
and does not meet the requirements to science. To seek
understanding without reflection and to resort to the
rules of understanding only in special cases is an unbal-
anced operation. Since one cannot do without either
of these two standpoints, one must combine them. This

1. Hermeneutics deals only with the art of understanding, not with the presentation of what has been
understood. The presentation of what has been understood would be only one special part of the art of
speaking and writing, and that part could be done only
by relying upon general principles.

2. Nor is hermeneutics concerned exclusively with
difficult passages of texts written in foreign languages. To the contrary, it presupposes a familiarity
with both the contents and the language of a text.
Assuming such familiarity, difficulties with particular passages of a text arise only because the easier
ones have not been understood. Only an artistically
sound understanding can follow what is being said and
written.

3. It is commonly believed that by following general
principles one can trust one's common sense. But if
that is so, by following special principles, one can
trust one's natural instincts.

2. It is very difficult to assign general hermeneutics
its proper place among the sciences.

1. For a long time it was treated as an appendix to
Logic, but since Logic is no longer seen as dealing
with applied matters, this can no longer be done. The
philosopher per se has no interest in developing hermeneutical theory. He seldom works at understanding,
because he believes that it occurs by necessity.[2]

---

occurs in two ways: (1) Even where we think we can proceed
in an inartistic way we often encounter unexpected difficulties, the clues for the solution of which may be found
in the materials already passed over. Therefore, we are
always forced to pay attention to what may be able to resolve these problems. (2) If we always proceed artistically, we come at the end to an unconscious application of
the rules, without ever having been inartistic.

2. Moreover, philology has become positivistic.
Thus its way of treating hermeneutics results in a
mere aggregate of observations.

3. Since the art of speaking and the art of understanding
stand in relation to each other, speaking being only the
outer side of thinking, hermeneutics is a part of the art
of thinking, and is therefore philosophical.*

1. Yet these two are to be related in such a way that
the art of interpretation at once depends upon and
presupposes composition. They are parallel in the
sense that artless speaking does not require any art
to be understood.

II. 4. Speaking is the medium for the communality of
thought, and for this reason rhetoric and hermeneutics belong together and both are related to dialectics.

1. Indeed, a person thinks by means of speaking.
Thinking matures by means of internal speech, and to
that extent speaking is only developed thought. But
whenever the thinker finds it necessary to fix what he
has thought, there arises the art of speaking, that
is, the transformation of original internal speaking,
and interpretation becomes necessary.
2. Hermeneutics and rhetoric are intimately related
in that every act of understanding is the reverse side
of an act of speaking, and one must grasp the thinking
that underlies a given statement.
3. Dialectics relies on hermeneutics and rhetoric because the development of all knowledge depends on both
speaking and understanding.

5. Just as every act of speaking is related to both the
totality of the language and the totality of the speaker's

---

*General hermeneutics is related to criticism as well as
to grammar. And since there can be no communication or
even acquisition of knowledge without all three, and since
all correct thinking is based on correct speaking, all
three are related to dialectics. Now 5 can follow.

thoughts, so understanding a speech always involves two
moments: to understand what is said in the context of the
language with its possibilities, and to understand it as a
fact in the thinking of the speaker.*

1. Every act of speaking presupposes a given language. This statement could also be reversed, not only for the absolutely first act of speaking in a language, but also for its entire history, because language develops through speaking. In every case communication presupposes a shared language and therefore
some knowledge of the language. Whenever something
comes between the internal speaking and its communication, one must turn to the art of speaking. So the
art of speaking is due in part to a speaker's anxiety
that something in his use of language may be unfamiliar to the hearer.

2. Every act of speaking is based on something having
been thought. This statement, too, could be reversed,
but with respect to communication the first formulation holds because the art of understanding deals only
with an advanced stage of thinking.

3. Accordingly, each person represents one locus
where a given language takes shape in a particular
way, and his speech can be understood only in the context of the totality of the language. But then too he
is a person who is a constantly developing spirit, and
his speaking can be understood as only one moment in
this development in relation to all others.

6. Understanding takes place only in the coinherence of
these two moments.

---

*3. Explanation of 5 and 6
How grammatical and psychological interpretation are related to dialectical and rhetorical thinking.
Each makes use of the other. Grammatical and psychological remain the main divisions.

1. An act of speaking cannot even be understood as a
moment in a person's development unless it is also understood in relation to the language. This is because
the linguistic heritage [Angeborenheit der Sprache]
modifies the spirit.

2. Nor can an act of speaking be understood as a modification of the language unless it is also understood
as a moment in the development of the person (later
addition: because an individual is able to influence a
language by speaking, which is how a language develops.)

III. 7. These two hermeneutical tasks are completely
equal, and it would be incorrect to label grammatical interpretation the "lower" and psychological interpretation
the "higher" task.*

1. Psychological interpretation is higher when one
regards the language exclusively as a means by which a
person communicates his thoughts. Then grammatical
interpretation is employed only to clear away initial
difficulties.

2. Grammatical interpretation and language, because
it conditions the thinking of every person, are higher
only when one regards the person and his speaking exclusively as occasions for the language to reveal itself. Then psychological interpretation and the life
of the individual become subordinate considerations.

3. From this dual relation it is evident that the two
tasks are completely equal.

---

*On 7. There is no way to distinguish between what is
easy or difficult in general terms. Rather, to one person
the one task is easier; to another, the other. Consequently, there are two different main approaches and main
works, notes on language and introductions.
4. Continuation of 7. Neither task is higher than the
other. 6, 8, 9.

8. The task is finally resolved when either side could be replaced by the other, though both must be treated, that is to say, when each side is treated in such a way that the treatment of the other side produces no change in the result.

1. Both grammatical and psychological interpretation must be treated, even though either can substitute for the other, in accordance with II, 6.

2. Each side is complete only when it makes the other superfluous and contributes to its work. This is because language can be learned only by understanding what is spoken, and because the inner make-up of a person, as well as the way in which external objects affect him, can only be understood from his speaking.

9. Interpretation is an art.

1. Each side is itself an art. For each side constructs something finite and definite from something infinite and indefinite. Language is infinite because every element is determinable in a special way by the other elements.

This statement also applies to psychological interpretation, for every intuition of a person is itself infinite. Moreover, external influences on a person will have ramifications which trail off into infinity. Such a construction, however, cannot be made by means of rules which may be applied with self-evident certainty.

2. In order to complete the grammatical side of interpretation it would be necessary to have a complete knowledge of the language. In order to complete the psychological side it would be necessary to have a complete knowledge of the person. Since in both cases such complete knowledge is impossible, it is necessary to move back and forth between the grammatical and psychological sides, and no rules can stipulate exactly how to do this.

10.   The success of the art of interpretation depends on
one's linguistic competence and on one's ability for knowing people.

1.   By "linguistic competence" I am not referring to a
facility for learning foreign languages. The distinction between one's mother tongue and a foreign language is not at issue here. Rather, I refer to one's
command of language, one's sensitivity to its similarities and differences, etc. --It could be claimed
that in this respect rhetoric and hermeneutics must
always belong together. But hermeneutics requires one
kind of competence, rhetoric requires another, and the
two are not the same. To be sure, both hermeneutics
and rhetoric require linguistic competence, but hermeneutics makes use of that competence in a different
way.

2.   One's ability to know people refers especially to
a knowledge of the subjective element determining the
composition of thoughts. Thus, just as with hermeneutics and rhetoric, so with hermeneutics and the artful
description of persons, there is no permanent connection. Nonetheless, many errors in hermeneutics are
due to a lack of this talent or to a flaw in its application.

3.   Insofar as these abilities are universal gifts of
nature, hermeneutics is everybody's concern. To the
extent that a person is deficient in one of these talents, he is hampered, and the other gift can do no
more than help him choose wisely from the suggestions
made by others.

IV.   11.   The art of interpretation is not equally interested in every act of speaking. Some instances fail to
spark its interest at all, while others engage it

completely. Most, however, fall somewhere between these
two extremes.*

1. A statement may be regarded to be of no interest
when it is neither important as a human act nor significant for the language. It is said because the
language maintains itself only by constant repetition.
But that which is only already available and repeated
is itself of no significance. Conversations about the
weather. But these statements are not absolutely de-
void of significance, since they may be said to be
"minimally significant," in that they are constructed
in the same way as more profound statements.

2. A statement may be of maximum significance for one
side of interpretation or the other. It is maximally
significant for the grammatical side when it is lin-
guistically creative to an exceptional degree and minimally repetitive: classical texts. A statement is
maximally significant for the psychological side when
it is highly individualized and minimally commonplace:
original texts. The term "absolute" is reserved for

---

*Hour 5. 10-11.
On 11. Of minimal worth is such common speech as (a)
business discussions [geschäftliche] and (b) conversations. Of maximal worth, predominately for language:
(a) original [urbildlich] for the production of thoughts =
too much. Those types of speech between these two extremes lie closer to one extreme or the other--(a) toward
common speech, that is, with a relatively important subject matter and a graceful presentation; (b) toward creative [geniale] speech, the classical quality of the language need not be original, and the originality in the
combination of elements need not be classical.
A great deal of talent is necessary not only to deal with
difficult passages, but also in order not to be content
with an immediate purpose, and to pursue both directions
in order to reach the goal.

statements that achieve a maximum of both linguistic
creativity and individuality: works of genius [das
Genialische].

3. "Classical" and "original" statements cannot be
transitory, but must be definitive for later productions. Indeed, even absolute texts are influenced to
some degree by earlier and more common ones.

12. Although both sides of interpretation should always
be applied, they will always be weighted differently.*

[1]. This is because a statement that is grammatically insignificant is not necessarily psychologically
insignificant and vice versa. Thus, in dealing with a
text that is in one respect insignificant, we cannot
reach what is significant in it by applying both sides
equally.

2. A minimum of psychological interpretation is appropriate when what is to be interpreted is predominately objective. Pure history, especially in its details, whereas the overall viewpoint requires more
psychological interpretation since it is always subjectively affected. Epics. Commercial records that
can be used as historical sources. Didactic treatments in the strict sense on every subject. In such
cases the subjective is not applied as a moment of interpretation, but results from the interpretation. A
minimum of grammatical interpretation in conjunction
with a maximum of psychological is appropriate in
dealing with letters, especially personal letters.
There is a point of transition along the continuum
from historical and didactic pieces to personal letters. Lyric poetry. Polemics?

13. There are no methods of interpretation other than
those discussed above.

1. For example, in the dispute over the historical
interpretation of the New Testament there emerged the

---

*6. 12 and 13 were begun.

curious view that there are several different kinds of
interpretation. To the contrary, only historical interpretation can do justice to the rootedness of the
New Testament authors in their time and place. (Awk-
ward expressions. Concepts of time.) But historical
interpretation is wrong when it denies Christianity's
power to create new concepts and attempts to explain
it in terms of conditions which were already present
in the time. It is proper to reject such a one-sided
historical interpretation, but it is improper to reject historical interpretation altogether.[3] The crux
of the matter, then, lies in the relationship between
grammatical and psychological interpretation, since
new concepts developed from the distinctive manner in
which the authors were affected.

V. 2. Historical interpretation is not to be limited
to gathering historical data. That task should be
done even before interpretation begins, since it is
the means for re-creating the relationship between the
speaker and the original audience, and interpretation
cannot begin until that relationship has been established.

3. Allegorical interpretation does not deal with allegories where the figurative meaning is the only one
intended, regardless of whether the stories are based
on truth, as in the parable of the sower, or on fic-
tion, as in the parable of the rich man,[4] but to cases
where the literal meaning, in its immediate context,
gives rise to a second, figurative meaning. Such instances cannot be dismissed by citing the general
principle that a given passage can have only one meaning, that is, its usual grammatical one.[5] Allusions
always involve a second meaning, and if a reader does
not catch this second meaning along with the first, he
misses one of the intended meanings, even though he
may be able to follow the literal one. At the same
time, to claim that there is an allusion where there

actually is none is also an error. An allusion occurs
when an additional meaning is so entwined with the
main train of thought that the author believes it
would be easily recognized by another person. These
additional meanings are not merely occasional and unimportant, but just as the whole world is posited ide-
ally in man, it is always considered real, although
only as a dark shadow-image. There is a parallelism
of different stages [Reihen] in the large and the
small, and therefore there can occur in any one something from another: parallelism of the physical and
the ethical of music and painting. But these paral-
lelisms are to be noted only when figurative expressions indicate them. There is a special reason why
parallelism occurs without clues, especially in Homer
and in the Bible.* VI. This accounts for the singu-

---

*Hour 7. Continuation of 13.
In the search for what is rich in meaning and significance, dogmatic and allegorical interpretations share the
common assumptions that the result should be as rich as
possible for Christian doctrine and that nothing in the
Holy Scriptures should be seen to be insignificant or of
merely passing significance.[6]
Move from this discussion to the question of inspiration.
Given the great variety of ideas of inspiration, it is
best, first of all, to test what sort of consequences the
strictest idea leads to, i.e., the idea that the power of
the spirit extends from the inception of the thought to
the act of writing itself. Due to the variants, this no
longer helps us. These were, however, already present before the Scriptures were collected. Here, too, then,
criticism is necessary. --But even the first readers of
the apostles' epistles would have had to abstract from
their ideas to the author and from the application of
their knowledge of that, and would have become completely
confused. If one then asks why the Scriptures did not

larity of Homer as a book for general education and of
the Old Testament as a body of literature from which
everything is to be drawn. To this it should be added
that the mythical contents in both are developed into
esoteric [gnomische] philosophy on the one hand and
into history on the other. But there is no technical
interpretation for myth because it cannot be traced
back to a single person, and the shifting in ordinary
understanding between the literal and figurative meanings draws out the double meaning most clearly. In
the case of the New Testament, however, the situation
was quite different, and a method based on two principles was developed. First, in keeping with the close
connection between the two testaments, the type of explanation used in interpreting the Old Testament was
applied to the New Testament as well, and this type of
interpretation was carried over into scholarly interpretations. The second principle was the idea, more
thoroughly applied to the New Testament than to the
Old, that the Holy Spirit was the author. Since the
Holy Spirit could not be conceived as an individual
consciousness that changed in time, there arose a tendency to find everything in each part.[7] Universal

---

arise in a totally miraculous way without the involvement
of humans, we must answer that the divine spirit can have
chosen the method it did only if it wanted everything
traced back to the declared author. Therefore, this interpretation must be correct. The same point holds with
respect to the grammatical side. But then every element
must be treated as purely human, and the action of the
Spirit was only to produce the inner impulse.
Other views, ascribing some special trait to the spirit
(e.g., protection from error) but not others, are untenable. For example, protection from error means that the
process of writing is hedged in, but putting down what is
right in a given place devolves on the author.

truths or particular instructions satisfy this inclination, but the results which are produced are in the
main unconnected and, taken in isolation, insignificant.

4. Incidentally, the question arises whether on account of the Holy Spirit the Scriptures must be treated in a special way. This question cannot be answered
by a dogmatic decision about inspiration, because such
a decision itself depends upon interpretation.

1. We must not make a distinction between what
the apostles spoke and what they wrote, for the
church had to be built on their speeches.

2. But for this reason we must not suppose that
their writings were addressed to all of Christendom, for in fact each text was addressed to specific people, and their writings could not be
properly understood in the future unless these
first readers could understand them. But these
first readers would have looked for what was specifically related to their own situations, and
from this material they had to derive the whole
truth of Christianity. Our interpretation must
take this fact into account, and we must assume
that even if the authors had been merely passive
tools of the Holy Spirit, the Holy Spirit could
have spoken through them only as they themselves
would have spoken.*[8]

---

*8. Whether the view that everything in the Scriptures
was inspired means that everything must relate to the
whole church? No. This view would necessarily entail
that the original recipients would interpret them incor-
rectly, so that it would have been better if the Holy
Spirit had not produced the Scriptures as occasional writings. Therefore, grammatical and psychological interpretation always proceed in accord with the general rules.
To what extent a specialized hermeneutics is still required cannot be discussed until later.

VII. 5. The worst offender in this respect is caba-
listic interpretation which labors to find everything
in the particular elements and their signs.[9] --One
sees that whatever efforts can be legitimately called
interpretation, there are no other types except those
based on the different relationships between the two
sides we have noted.

14. The distinction between artful and artless interpretation is not based on the difference between what is familiar to us and what is unfamiliar, or between what is
spoken and what is written. Rather, it is based on the
fact that we want to understand with precision some things
and not others.*

1. Were the art of interpretation needed only for
foreign and ancient texts, then the original readers
obviously would not have required it.[10] Were this the
case, then in effect the art of interpretation would
be based on the differences between the original readers and us. But historical and linguistic knowledge
removes that obstacle, and so only after significant
points of comparison between the first readers and us
have been reached can interpretation begin. Therefore, the only difference between ancient and foreign
texts and contemporary texts in our own language is
that the comparisons necessary for interpreting the
former cannot be completed prior to the interpretation
but begins and is completed with the process of interpretation. As he works the interpreter should keep
this fact in mind.

---

*14-16. We stand at the point of total opposition between
artless and artful interpretation. If one moves to the
latter only when difficulties are encountered, one will
come to no more than discrete observations. --Precise understanding means that one grasps the easy parts of the
meaning and uses them as a key for interpreting the difficult parts.

2. Nor do written texts alone call for the art of interpretation. Were that true, the art would be necessary only because of the difference between written
and spoken words, that is, because of the loss of the
living voice and the absence of supplementary personal
impressions. But the latter must themselves be interpreted, and that interpretation is never certain. To
be sure, the living voice facilitates understanding,
and a writer must take this fact into consideration.
Were he to do so, then, on the assumption that the art
of interpretation is not necessary for oral statements, the art would not be necessary for his written
text. But that simply is not the case. Therefore,
even if an author did not consider the effects of the
living voice, the necessity for the art of interpretation is not based on the difference between oral and
written statements.*

3. Given this relationship between speaking and writing, the distinction between artful and artless interpretation must be based on nothing else than the principle stated above, and it follows that artistic interpretation has the same aim as we do in ordinary
listening.

VIII. 15. There is a less rigorous practice of this art
which is based on the assumption that understanding occurs
as a matter of course. The aim of this practice may be
expressed in negative form as: "misunderstanding should be
avoided."

1. This less rigorous practice presupposes that it
deals mainly with insignificant matters or that it has
a quite specific interest, and so it establishes limited, easily realizable goals.

---

*That the art is necessary more for spoken than written
language, because as the speech is spoken one cannot remember the various rules which are to be used.

2. Even here, however, difficulties may necessitate recourse to artful interpretation. In this way hermeneutics originated from artless practice. But because it was applied only to difficult cases, it produced merely a collection of observations. At the same time this practice gave rise to special hermeneutics, since difficult passages could be more easily worked out within a delimited framework. Both theological and juristic hermeneutics arose in this way,[11] and even the philologists have pursued only specialized aims.

3. In short, the less rigorous practice is based on the fact that the speaker and hearer share a common language and a common way of formulating thoughts.

16. There is a more rigorous practice of the art of interpretation that is based on the assumption that misunderstanding occurs as a matter of course, and so understanding must be willed and sought at every point.

1. This more rigorous practice consists in grasping the text precisely with the understanding and in viewing it from the standpoint of both grammatical and psychological interpretation.

(Note: It is common experience that one notices no distinction until . . [the] beginning of a misunderstanding.)

2. Therefore, this more rigorous practice presupposes that the speaker and hearer differ in their use of language and in their ways of formulating thoughts, although to be sure there is an underlying unity between them. This is one of the less significant matters overlooked by artless interpretation.*

---

*9. Discuss the difference (πίστις) between the subjective in artistic interpretation and the objective as such.

17. Both qualitative misunderstanding of the contents of
a work and quantitative misunderstanding of its tone are
to be avoided.*

1. Objective qualitative misunderstanding occurs when
one part of speech in the language is confused with
another, as for example, when the meanings of two
words are confused. Subjective qualitative misunderstanding occurs when the reference of an expression is
confused.

2. Subjective quantitative misunderstanding occurs
when one misses the potential power of development of
a part of speech or the value given it by the speaker.
Analogous to this, objective quantitative misunderstanding occurs when one mistakes the degree of importance which a part of speech has.

3. From quantitative misunderstanding, which usually
receives less consideration, qualitative always
develops.

4. This thesis (17) encompasses the full task of interpretation, but because it is stated negatively we
cannot develop rules from it. In order to develop
rules we must work from a positive thesis, but we must
constantly be oriented to this negative formulation.

5. We must also distinguish between passive and active misunderstanding. The latter occurs when one
reads something into a text because of one's own bias.
In such a case the author's meaning cannot possibly
emerge.**

IX. 18. The rules for the art of interpretation must be
developed from a positive formula, and this is: "the historical and divinatory, objective and subjective reconstruction of a given statement."

---

*17. Negative formulation of the task: to avoid misunder-
standing the material and formal elements.

**Hour 10. 17,5. This represents the maximum, because it
is caused by completely false presuppositions. --18. 19.

1. "Objective-historical" means to consider the statement in [its] relation to the language as a whole, and to consider the knowledge it contains as a product of the language. --"Objective-prophetic" means to sense how the statement itself will stimulate further developments in the language. Only by taking both of these aspects into account can qualitative and quantitative misunderstanding be avoided.

2. "Subjective-historical" means to know how the statement, as a fact in the person's mind, has emerged. "Subjective-prophetic" means to sense how the thoughts contained in the statement will exercise further influence on and in the author. Here, again, unless both of these aspects are taken into account, qualitative and quantitative misunderstandings are unavoidable.

3. The task is to be formulated as follows: "To understand the text at first as well as and then even better than its author." Since we have no direct knowledge of what was in the author's mind, we must try to become aware of many things of which he himself may have been unconscious, except insofar as he reflects on his own work and becomes his own reader. Moreover, with respect to the objective aspects, the author had no data other than we have.[12]

4. So formulated, the task is infinite, because in a statement we want to trace a past and a future which stretch into infinity. Consequently, inspiration is as much a part of this art as of any other. Inasmuch as a text does not evoke such inspiration, it is insignificant. --The question of how far and in which directions interpretation will be pressed must be decided in each case on practical grounds. Specialized hermeneutics and not general hermeneutics must deal with these questions.

19.   Before the art of hermeneutics can be practiced, the interpreter must put himself both objectively and subjectively in the position of the author.

1. On the objective side this requires knowing the language as the author knew it. But this is a more specific task than putting oneself in the position of the original readers, for they, too, had to identify with the author. On the subjective side this requires knowing the inner and the outer aspects of the author's life.

2. These two sides can be completed only in the interpretation itself. For only from a person's writings can one learn his vocabulary, and so, too, his character and his circumstances.

20.   The vocabulary and the history of an author's age together form a whole from which his writings must be understood as a part, and vice versa.

1. Complete knowledge always involves an apparent circle, that each part can be understood only out of the whole to which it belongs, and vice versa. All knowledge which is scientific must be constructed in this way.

2. To put oneself in the position of an author means to follow through with this relationship between the whole and the parts. Thus it follows, first, that the more we learn about an author, the better equipped we are for interpretation, but, second, that a text can never be understood right away. On the contrary, every reading puts us in a better position to understand because it increases our knowledge. Only in the case of insignificant texts are we satisfied with what we understand on first reading.

X.   21. An interpreter who gains all his knowledge of an author's vocabulary from lexical aids and disconnected

114

observations can never reach an independent interpretation.*

1. The only source independent of interpretation for knowing an author's vocabulary is the immediate, living heritage of the language. With Greek and Latin that source is incomplete. This is why the first lexicographical works, which searched the whole literature in order to learn about the language, were put together. Consequently, these dictionaries must be constantly emended by interpretation itself, and every artful interpretation must contribute to that end.

2. By the "vocabulary" of an author I include the dialect, sentence structure, and type of language characteristic of a given genre, the latter beginning with the distinction between poetry and prose.

3. Various aids may be indispensable for a beginner's first steps, but an independent interpretation demands that the interpreter acquire his background knowledge through independent research. All of the information about a language which dictionaries and other resource works supply represents the product of particular and often questionable interpretations.

4. In New Testament studies, especially, it can be said that the questionableness and arbitrariness of interpretation is due in large measure to this failure. For references to particular observations can lead to contradictory results. --The road to comprehending the language of the New Testament leads one from classical antiquity through (a) Macedonian Greek, (b) the Jewish secular writers (Josephus and Philo), (c) the deuterocanonical writings, and (d) the Septuagint, which is closest to Hebrew.

---

*Hour 11. 19, 20, 21, 22. I only began 22. Neither 21 nor 22 were applied to the New Testament.
Hour 12. Apply 21 and 22 to the New Testament.

22. An interpreter who gains his historical knowledge
solely from prolegomena cannot reach an independent interpretation.

    1. Any editor who wants to be helpful should provide
such prolegomena, in addition to the usual critical
aids. Preparing such prolegomena requires a knowledge
of the whole circle of literature to which a writing
belongs and of everything that has been written about
a given author. For this reason these prolegomena
themselves depend on interpretation, and . . at the
same time how they were compiled may be irrelevant to
the aim of the reader. The precise interpreter, however, must gradually derive all of his conclusions
from the sources themselves. Thus he must proceed
from the easier to the more difficult passages. A dependence on prolegomena is most damaging when one
takes conclusions from them that should have been derived from the original sources.

    2. In New Testament studies a separate discipline has
been created to deal with this background information,
the Introduction. The Introduction is not truly an
organic part of the theological sciences, but it does
serve a practical purpose for both the beginner and
the master, because it is helpful to have all the previous research on a given topic collected in one
place. But the interpreter must contribute to extending and verifying this information.

The various ways of arranging and using this fragmentary background information have given rise to different, but also one-sided, schools of interpretation,
which can easily be branded as fads [als manier].

XI. 23. Also within each given text, its parts can only
be understood in terms of the whole, and so the interpreter must gain an overview of the work by a cursory reading
before undertaking a more careful interpretation.

1. Here, too, there seems to be a circle. This provisional understanding requires only that knowledge of the particulars which comes from a general knowledge of the language.

2. Synopses provided by the author are too sparse to serve the purpose of even technical interpretation. and the summaries which editors customarily give in prolegomena bring the reader under the power of their own interpretations.

3. The interpreter should seek to identify the leading ideas by which all the others are to be assessed. Likewise, in technical interpretation, one should try to identify the basic train of thought by reference to which particular ideas may be more readily recognized. That these tasks are indispensable for both technical and grammatical interpretation can be easily seen from the various types of misunderstanding.

4. It is not necessary to gain an overview of insignificant texts, and although an overview seems to offer little help in dealing with difficult texts, it is nonetheless indispensable. It is characteristic of difficult authors that an overview is of little help.*

Whenever we are actually engaged in the interpretation of a particular text, we must always hold the two sides of interpretation together. But in setting forth the theory of hermeneutics we must separate them and discuss the two separately. Nonetheless, each side of interpretation must be developed so thoroughly that the other becomes dispen-

---

*13. 23. General rule for the method: (a) Begin with a general overview of the text. (b) Comprehend it by moving in both directions simultaneously. (c) Only when the two coincide for one passage does one proceed to another passage. (d) When the two do not agree, it is necessary to go back until the error in calculation is found.

sable, or, better, that the results of the two coincide.
Grammatical interpretation comes first.

Part 1: Grammatical Interpretation

XII. 1. First canon: A more precise determination of any
point in a given text must be decided on the basis of the
use of language common to the author and his original
public.

1. Every point needs to be more precisely defined,
and that determination is first of all provided by the
context. Considered in isolation, every element of
language, both formal and material, is indefinite.
For any given word or linguistic form we can conceive
a certain range [Cyclus] of usages.

2. Some term what a word is thought to mean "in and
of itself" its meaning [Bedeutung] and what the word
is thought to mean in a given context its "sense"
[Sinn]. Others argue that a word can have only a single meaning [Bedeutung] and not a sense [Sinn]; that a
sentence regarded in isolation has a sense [Sinn], but
not a purport [Verstand], for only a complete text has
a purport.[13] Of course, it could be claimed that even
a whole text would be more completely understood in
the context of its entire world, but this consideration leads us beyond the sphere of interpretation altogether. --The latter terminology is certainly pre-
ferable inasmuch as a sentence is an inseparable unity
and as such its sense [Sinn] is also a unity, that is,
there is a mutual co-determination of its subject and
predicate. Nonetheless, this terminology is not adequate to linguistic usage. For with reference to the
purport [Verstand] of a text, and meaning and sense
are identical. The truth is that in interpretation
the task of clarifying what is vague is never-ending.
--When a given sentence is a self-enclosed whole, the
distinction between sense and purport seems to disappear, as in the case of epigrams and maxims. This

whole, however, must be determined by the reader: each
reader has to puzzle through such statements as best
he can. The meaning is decided by reference to the
particular subject matter.

3. The era in which an author lives, his development,
his involvements, his way of speaking--whenever these
factors make a difference is a finished text--consti-
tute his "sphere." But this sphere cannot be found in
toto in every text, for it varies according to the
kind of reader the author had in mind. But how do we
determine who these readers were? Only by a cursory
reading of the entire text. But determining the
sphere common to the author and the readers is only
the first step. It must be continued throughout the
process of interpretation, and it is completed only
when the interpretation itself is concluded.

4. There are several apparent exceptions to the rule.

   a. Archaic expressions lie beyond the immediate
   linguistic sphere of the author and his readers.
   They serve the purpose of making the past contemporaneous with the present; they are used in writing more than in speaking, in poetry more than in
   prose.

   b. Technical expressions occur in even the most
   common forms of speaking, as, for example, in le-
   gal proceedings, even though not everyone understands them. This fact leads us to observe that
   an author does not always have his entire public
   in mind, but only certain sectors of it. Consequently, the application of this rule requires a
   certain amount of art, since it depends on the interpreter's sensitivity [richtige Gefühle].[14]

XIV. 5. The statement that we must consciously grasp
an author's linguistic sphere, in contrast to other
organic aspects of his language, implies that we understand the author better than he understood himself.
Both in our general survey and in our work on particular passages difficulties arise, and we must become

aware of many things of which the author himself was
unaware.[15]

6. By drawing on our general survey of the work, interpretation may continue smoothly for some time without actually being artless, because everything is held
together in a general picture. But as soon as some
detail causes us difficulty, we begin to wonder whether the problem lies with the author or with us. We
may assume that the author is at fault only when our
overview of the text uncovers evidence that the author
is careless and imprecise, or confused and without
talent. Our own errors may be caused in two ways. We
may have made an early mistake in understanding that
had continued unnoticed, or our knowledge of the language might be inadequate. In either case, the correct word usage does not occur to us. I will discuss
the former later, because it is related to the use of
parallel passages. I want to discuss the latter now.

7. Dictionaries, which are the normal resources for
supplementing our knowledge of a language, view the
various usages of a word as a many-faceted, loosely-
bound aggregate. They do not trace the meaning
[Bedeutung] back to its original unity, because to do
so would require that the material be arranged according to the system of concepts, and this is impossible.
The multiplicity of meanings, then, is to be analyzed
into a series of distinctions. The first is the distinction between the literal and the figurative. Upon
closer scrutiny this distinction disappears. In sim-
iles two parallel series of thoughts are connected.
Each word stands in its own series and should be determined only in those terms. Therefore, it retains
its own meaning. In metaphors this connection is only
suggested, and often only a single aspect of the concept is emphasized. For example, coma arborum is
foliage, but coma still means hair.[16] And we speak of
the lion as the king of the animals. But a lion does

not govern, and kings are not entitled to devour others on the principle that "might makes right." Such a
single usage of the word has no meaning, and usually
the entire phrase must be given. This distinction may
be ultimately traced to the belief and not all non-
literal [geistliche] meanings are original, but that
they are imagistic usages of words that had sense-
referents. XV. But this question lies beyond the
sphere of hermeneutics. Even if θεός (God) is derived
from θέω, this fact would not be immediately evident
in the language because it arose in the primitive history of the language, with which hermeneutics does not
deal. The question is whether non-literal ideas
[geistliche Vorstellungen] are a second stage of development that does not begin until after the language
has been formed, and there does not seem to be any answer to that question. It is undeniable that there
are non-literal words which at the same time signify
sense-objects, but a parallelism governs these cases
in that both, as they present themselves to us, are
included in the idea of one living whole. This accounts, too, for the use of the same words for matters
relating to space and time. The two meanings are essentially the same because we can determine space only
by reference to time, and vice versa. Terms for form
and movement are also interchangeable, and so a
"creeping plant" is not a figurative expression.[17]
There are just as many problems with the distinction
between original and derived meanings. In Latin
hostis originally meant "stranger," but it came to
mean "enemy." Originally all strangers were enemies.
Later it became possible to be friendly with foreign-
ers, and people instinctively decided that the word
had referred more to a difference of disposition than
to a distance of space. One could therefore speak of
certain fellow citizens as hostes [enemies], but perhaps only those who had been exiled. People also make

a distinction between general and specific meanings,
the former occuring in ordinary conversation and the
latter in special areas of discussion. Often these
meanings are basically the same, or elliptical. Thus,
the word "foot" stands for a measurement of length or
a unit of poetry, or for a step, or a step forward.
The difference between general and particular meanings, then, develops because the terminology used in a
special discipline takes on a more general meaning
when used by groups of people who do not understand it
precisely. Frequently, too, foreign words become gar-
bled and remolded until they seem to be native words.
All of the other distinctions about word-meanings
arise in similar ways.

8. The basic task, even for dictionaries designed
specifically for interpreters, is to identify the true
and complete unity of a given word. Of course, the
occurrence of a word in a given passage involves an
infinite, indeterminate multiplicity. The only way to
grasp the unity of a word within such a multiplicity
of usages is to consider the multiplicity as a clearly
circumscribed grouping with a unity of its own. Such
a unity in turn must break up into distinctions. But
a word is never isolated, even when it occurs by itself, for its determination is not derived from itself, but from its context. We need only to relate
this contextual use to this original unity in order to
discover the correct meaning in each case. But to
find the complete unity of a word would be to explain
it, and that is as difficult as completely explaining
objects. The elements of dead languages cannot be
fully explained because we are not yet in a position
to trace their whole development, and those of living
languages cannot be explained because they are still
developing.

XVI. 9. Granting that a multiplicity of usages is
possible with an existing unity, then a multiplicity

must already be present in the unity: several major points are bound together as variables within certain limits. One's linguistic sense must be attentive to this, and when uncertainties arise, reference to a dictionary can help orient us to what is known about the word. The various instances cited in the dictionary should be regarded merely as a reasonable selection. One must connect the various citations in order to bring into view the full range of the word and to determine the meaning of a given usage.

10. The same holds for the formal element. The rules of grammar are just like the meanings cited in a dictionary. Thus, in dealing with particles, a grammar serves as a dictionary. It is even more difficult, however, to deal with the formal elements of the language.

11. To use these aids is in effect to make use of another author, and so all of the rules of interpretation apply here as well. These two resources represent only a certain segment of our knowledge of a language, and usually each is written from a definite point of view. Therefore, in the use of these aids a scholar will make corrections and additions in order to reach a better understanding. All of his work should contribute to this end.

2. Application to the New Testament

1. The special hermeneutics of the New Testament has to be constructed from a group of things that are not yet exactly known to us. In general a special hermeneutics is only an abbreviated procedure which must be governed by the general rules. But when the special hermeneutics degenerates into a collection of observations, then this abbreviation has been made at the expense of its scientific character and so, too, of its certainty. Consequently, a special hermeneutics must be constructed in an orderly way, so that at every point attention is directed to what the given

object of inquiry allows or excludes. --Each language could have its own special hermeneutics if we were to construe it in its special character from the idea of language as such and to compare it with other languages. But we are unable to do this. Yet all languages pass through three stages of development: origin, maturity, and decay. In every language, each of these stages displays a special character. As a parallel to the investigation of these special characters, however, we must consider the transition to technical interpretation which treats the author's relation to the language and asks which is greater, his influence on the language or the influence of the language on him.

2. The language of the New Testament must be included within the overall development of the Greek language. The books themselves are not translations, not even The Gospel of Matthew and Hebrews. Nor did the authors think in Hebrew and write, or let someone else write for them, in Greek. They could assume that there were better translators among their readers. Like any intelligent person they thought in the language in which they wrote. (This applies, at least, to their detailed expositions, since we are not concerned with original conceptions that were never developed.) (Note: I understand the linguistic sphere of the New Testament to be comprised of the following: (1) the language of the Old Testament ("Job" and the Psalms), (2) Macedonian Greek, (3) translations from Hebrew, (4) Hellenistic Jewish writings (these vary according to their similarities to Philo and Josephus). In addition, we should inquire to what extent patristic Greek belongs to this same linguistic sphere.)

To what extent is patristic Greek to be included here.

3. The New Testament was composed during the period of decay in the Greek language. This decay can be

detected as early as the time of Alexander. To be
sure, a few writers attempt to equal or to reconstruct
the language of the classical period. But since the
writers of the New Testament made more use of the language of common life, they do not have this tendency.
But they too are to be included here whenever they
passively took over usages current in their own time.
Therefore, valid similarities may be found in Polybius
and Josephus. XVIII. Similarities with such Attic
authors as Thucydides and Xenophon have a negative
use, and it is a good practice to make such comparisons.[18] This practice serves to correct the common
view that the various spheres are totally separate and
that certain forms found in the New Testament could
not occur in classical Greek, but only in Hellenistic
and Macedonian Greek.

4. The extent to which Aramaic influenced the New
Testament must be determined on the basis of a general
conception of how a foreign language is appropriated.
Two forces are always present in a language: a tendency to preserve its native character and an inclination
to be of general use. Frequently the latter is only
minimal, but when it becomes predominant, the former
falls into decay. Of course, the ability to appropriate many languages skillfully by comparing the general
images found in one's native tongue with that found in
foreign languages is a talent. Though this talent was
never emphasized by the Jews, they had from the beginning a remarkable facility for appropriating other
languages, and it flourished among them up to the time
of the disappearance of their mother tongue. But in
the course of everyday communication, where grammar or
literature are ignored, there crept into this appropriation errors which would not be found among scholars. This is the difference between the New Testament
and Philo or Josephus. In the case of the New Testament these errors are of two sorts. First, due to the

contrast between the richness of formal elements in Greek and the poverty of Hebrew in this respect, the writers of the New Testament were unable to make full use of the richness of Greek. Secondly, since in the process of appropriation foreign words were translated into words in the native tongue, there easily arose the illusion that words corresponding in some respects correspond completely, and this assumption led to incorrect usages in their composition. Note. These errors occur in the Septuagint as well as the New Testament, and for this reason the Septuagint represents almost the best text available to us for clarifying the language of the New Testament. But it is going too far to say that the Septuagint is the source from which the language of the New Testament developed. First of all, just as the writers of the New Testament varied greatly in their appropriation of Greek and in their ability to appropriate it, so, too, all of them are dependent on another source, namely, the common language of their day.

XIX. 5. The extent to which the New Testament, because of its religious contents, depends in a special way on the Septuagint is an entirely different issue. Here we think especially of such earlier texts as the Apocrypha. Thus the answer to this question is of paramount importance for an overall view of Christian theology, namely, for the principles of interpretation insofar as they themselves are the bases for dogmatics. --The writers of the New Testament do not introduce any new words for their religious concepts, but speak from within the linguistic sphere of the Bible and Apocrypha. Nevertheless, the question remains as to whether or not they have different religious ideas and so use words in distinctive ways. If they do not, there would be nothing new in Christian theology, and, since every element of religion which is at all lasting becomes fixed as an object of reflection, there

would be nothing new in the Christian religion. Since
this question cannot be resolved immediately by means
of hermeneutics, it seems to be a matter of judgment
[Gesinnung]. Consequently, each person accuses the
other of having formed his principles from precon-
ceived ideas, because the correct meaning of the Bible
can be determined only by means of interpretation. In
the hermeneutical method there is a basis for overcoming this impasse. A thorough comparison of the New
Testament with the Apocrypha would certainly show if
the one contains usages that are entirely foreign to
the other. It could be stated in rebuttal that the
linguistic sphere is more encompassing than these
fragmentary materials. Therefore, we would have to
rely also on a judgment of feeling as to whether the
New Testament seems to develop new ideas. But judgments of feeling can be accepted only if they are supported by philological and philosophical research.
Only a person who has demonstrated his competence in
similar investigations concerning other matters and
bases his understanding on adequate study is worthy of
our trust in this research.

6. If we are correct in our view that Hebraic influences on the language of the New Testament were only
minor and anomalous, the question arises as to how
much attention is due these influences in interpreting
the New Testament. Two one-sided maxims are, first,
to focus exclusively on the one language until difficulties arise and, then, to attempt to overcome these
difficulties by referring to the other language. But
these maxims make the first procedure artless and ut-
terly unsuitable for being connected to the second.
Moreover, they make it too easy for one to attempt to
explain by the second moment something that has its
proper basis for explanation elsewhere, and in general
one is led back merely to isolated observations. But
in accord with our introductory rule that interpre-

tation must be "artful" from the very beginning, one
should try to develop a general conception of how
these two procedures are related, without reference to
particular difficulties in a text. This general conception should be formed by an initial perusal of the
New Testament and comparing it with the Septuagint,
Philo, Josephus, Diodorus, and Polybius.

XX. It cannot be denied that the Hebrew language exerted an especially strong influence on the religious
terminology of the New Testament. The original Hellenistic milieu, as the New Testament authors knew it,
did not offer them significant points of contact for
the newly developing religious ideas of their faith.
Indeed, these writers even rejected similar terms because they were associated with polytheism.

7. The result is a complex mixture of anomalies,
which varies with each writer. Therefore, the main
rule is that the interpreter should develop the whole
range of each word with the help of Greek and Hellenistic dictionaries and the whole range of each form
with the help of Greek and comparative Hellenistic
grammars. The canon should be applied only with reference to this procedure. --It is advisable for the
beginner to consult a bilingual dictionary even when
it does not seem necessary, so that all artless
practices can be avoided.

3. Second Canon. The meaning of each word of a passage
must be determined by the context in which it occurs.

1. The first canon serves only to exclude certain
possibilities. This second canon, however, seems to
be determinative, a "jump" which must be justified.

a. One moves from the first canon to the second.
Each word has a determinate linguistic sphere. In
explaining a word we use only what we believe can
be expected to occur with that linguistic sphere.
Similarly, the whole text more or less forms the
context and surroundings of each passage.

b.   Likewise, one moves from the second canon to
the first. When the given connection of subject,
predicate, and supplementary words is not sufficient to explain the meaning, one must turn to
other passages where these same words occur and,
under certain conditions, to other works of the
author or even to works written by others in which
these words appear. But one must always remain
within the same linguistic sphere.

2. Consequently, the distinction we have made between
the two canons, that the first is exclusive and the
second determinative, is more apparent than real. In
each particular case this second canon, too, only excludes certain possibilities. Every modifier excludes
a certain number of otherwise possible meanings, and
the determination of the word emerges by a process of
elimination. Since the application of this canon,
carried to its farthest extent, involves the entire
theory of parallel passages, these two canons comprise
the whole of grammatical interpretation.

XXI.   3. We must now discuss how to determine the
formal and material elements, and we must deal with
both in a way that draws on the immediate context and
on parallels, and aims at both qualitative and quantitative understanding. Either set of divisions may be
made the major basis for organizing the discussion.
But the first is the most natural, because it is a
two-way road that runs through the entire operation.

4. The use of parallel passages as a resource is only
an apparent extension of the canon, and the use of
parallel passages is limited by the canon. For a passage is "parallel" only when it can be considered,
with respect to the point in question, as identical
with the sentence itself, and so can be considered
part of a unified context.

5. Granting that the formal and material elements
constitute the major divisions of our discussion, it

is best to begin by considering how to determine the formal element, because our understanding of a given passage is related to our preliminary understanding of the whole, and the sentence is recognized as a unity only through the formal element.

4. On determining the formal element.*

We must divide formal elements into those that combine sentences and those that combine parts of speech to form a sentence.

1. At this point we must begin with the simple sentence, because combining individual statements into clauses and combining clauses to construct sentences are the same, whereas combining the parts of speech into a simple sentence is quite different. Included in the first are conjunctions and their rules, and whatever substitutes for them. Included in the second are prepositions.

The crux of the matter concerns the type of combination, its degree, and how much has been combined. In speech, as in everything else, there are only two types of combination, organic and mechanical, i.e., an inner fusion and an external adjoining of parts. This distinction, however, is not absolute, since one often seems to shade off into the other. Often a causal or adversative particle seems merely additive. In such cases it has lost or even abandoned its true content. But often an additive term becomes decisive, and it may then be said to have been enhanced or made emphatic. In this way a qualitative difference becomes quantitative. Often, however, this transposition is only apparent, and the interpreter must always refer back to the original meaning. Often, too, apparent transpositions are due to the fact that the extent or the object of the connection have not been correctly identified. Thus one should not decide

---

*1828. I have already dealt with the material element.

about a given case until all other questions have been considered.

XXII. a. An organic connection may be more or less cohesive, but one should never suppose that it has lost all its meaning, as is sometimes done when statements which have been combined do not seem to belong together. But (α) the last clause before the particle can be a mere addition, and therefore the connective terms refer back to the main clause. Or the first clause after the connective term may be merely introductory, such that the connection refers to the major thoughts which follow. Of course, in order to specify the extent of a given connection, these dependent clauses should be changed into parenthetical statements (Zwischensätze). The degree to which this procedure can be applied varies according to the style of the work. The more free the style, the more the author must rely on the reader. (β) Often, however, the connection does not refer to the last major thought but to a whole series of thoughts. Otherwise entire sections could not be connected. In writings with well-defined divisions, the points made in one section may be recapitulated in the course of moving to another, and the connection becomes an entire sentence which includes as well the main contents of the section which is to follow. More ponderous constructions may contain additions and repetitions, as well as elements that ought not be have been carried over. But even in more flowing constructions the reader must pay attention to the transitions. Therefore, a general overview of the text is doubly necessary before a given point can be understood.

b. That simply adjoining two statements can, as it were, become emphatic is due to the fact that

all our organic connective terms (<u>denn</u>; <u>weil</u>;
<u>wenn</u>) have evolved from particles that originally
related solely to space and time. Thus it becomes
possible that even today particles can be enhanced
in their meanings. The canon, then, is based on
the fact that one ought never presuppose that an
author has merely tacked the whole together. Mere
connection predominates in descriptions and narratives, but even there not completely, for this
would make the writer nothing more than a tran-
scriber. When the author is not a mere tran-
scriber, mere additions can only be in the service
of organic connections, that is, they are enclosed
in them, follow from them, or lead to them.
Therefore, even if no organic connection is evident, it must be implicit.[19]

XXIII. 5. Application to the New Testament

1. Even when a writer thinks in the language he uses,
he frequently relies on his mother tongue in conceiving the work. Moreover, the combination of thoughts
is already included in this initial conception, and so
special attention is to be directed to the mixture of
Hebrew and Greek.

2. This is all the more important because the two
languages are so different.

a. Due to their lack of education, the New Testament writers could not appropriate the richness of
the Greek language, nor could they by casual listening catch the significance of the different
types of connectives. Nonetheless, they sometimes
used these along with those they knew well.

b. Consequently, Greek signs which correspond in
certain respects were readily considered fully
equivalent.

3. It is therefore necessary to construct a whole
from the Greek meanings of a sign and from the corre-

sponding Hebraic ones and to make his judgment on this basis.

4. A loose style of writing permits extensive latitude in the use of these elements because the sentences themselves are joined together with little art.

5. The great differences among the New Testament writers in this respect are not to be overlooked. Paul works from the Greek most of all; John the least.

6. The reference works are poorly constructed for these purposes. It is especially important to refer to New Testament dictionaries in conjunction with dictionaries for the Septuagint. Above all, it is important to pay close attention ever to those passages that present no difficulties, for otherwise there is no way to assess the range of usages that are allowable. Failure to do this frequently causes errors.

7. Here I especially want to mention (for I forgot to include it under 4. a., above) that there are also subjective connections, namely, those that give reasons why something has previously been asserted. Since these combinations are indistinquishable in form from objective ones, they are often taken as a restriction of the meaning of a mere transition.

6. The problem of determining what parts of speech hold a sentence together is resolved by the interplay of several considerations.

1. In referring back to the general content, the leading ideas are of primary importance. In considering how the statements are put together, the subjects and predicates, in short, the material element, are the key.

2. In the immediate context the way in which the formal elements have been put together is the key; that is, the construction explains the particles, and vice versa.

3. In the succeeding material one must pay attention to coordinating and subordinating forms of combination.

4. The application must make good sense. The final
determination must always be based on a more impartial
reconstruction.

7. With respect to combinations within the sentence itself, the most difficult elements are the prepositions and
the parts of speech immediately dependent upon them.

1. It makes no difference whether the sentence consists of only a subject and predicate or has a copula
as well. In either case the immediate combination
should not be mistaken. Even when a sentence is expanded by means of adjectives and adverbs, it forms a
whole centered on its subject and predicate. The
preposition, however, gives the verb a more precise
determination, that is, it indicates how the object is
related to the verb. The genitive, <u>status construc-
tus</u>, provides a more precise determination of the subject. The meaning [<u>Sinn</u>] of a preposition is easily
determined by reference to the subject and object.
The material element is decisive.

2. In the New Testament Hebraicizing tendencies predominate. Therefore, the interpreter must always have
in mind the corresponding Hebrew forms.

8. Further remarks on combining sentences.

1. Unconnected sentences can occur only when a given
sentence is assumed to be united with the one that
precedes it, whether this be by a causal or merely
successive relation. In the former case the second
sentence is developed directly from the first, such
that its major point was already contained in the
first. In the latter case the two sentences are assumed to be coordinate. Mistakes are rare in this
matter.

2. In certain cases all of the conjunctions may sink
to enclitic insignificance. When that happens each
sentence is only vaguely suggestive of the other.

3. In dealing with an author who lacks critical consciousness, the connections themselves may seem to be
indeterminate.

4. In the interpretation of the New Testament all of
these problems converge. Both in the didactic writings which are governed by causal connections and in
the historical writings which are governed by narrative connections, the complexes of sentences are bound
together quite loosely, and often poor practices and
usages, due to a lack of knowledge, occur. For this
reason both types of writings are so difficult. Often
one cannot tell how far a didactic series or an historical account extends. Only Paul and John stand out
in this respect, Paul as a didactic writer and John as
an historical writer. The desire to be more definite
than the author himself depends on both dogmatic and
historical criticism. Thus, all of the philosophical
and critical difficulties must be solved by interpretation.

9. In some cases the problem can be traced to the material as well as the formal element.

For example, In Hebrew the hiphil and similar forms of
the verb can be taken as an inflection or as a separate word. This is also true of all derivative forms
of verbs and nouns, so that the difference between
them is not pure, but graduated. --In such cases the
interpreter must discover what kind of treatment provides a purer and richer whole within which to construe the meaning.

10. Subject and predicate are mutually determinative, but
not completely.

1. The mutual determination of subject and predicate
is most precise when a phrase has, in the technical
sense, a highly delimited and certain range. The
mutual determination is least precise when a subject
is combined with a seldomly used predicate that lies
outside of its normal range or when there is an

apophthegm [die Gnome] that offers no more precise
means of determination and so remains unclear, its
meaning being determined by the way it has been
applied.

11. Both subject and predicate are, singly and recipro-
cally, given more precise determination by their modifiers.

1. Adjectives and adverbs give nouns and verbs a certain tendency, and they rule out various possible
meanings. Even the parts of speech connected to the
verbs help to determine them more precisely, as is
evident from the fact that a preposition itself may
become a component of the verb.

2. But this consideration alone is not sufficient.
The positive, decisive element for determining the
subject and predicate is given only by reconstructing
the train of thought.

12. This task is of even greater importance for the New
Testament because of its new or unique concepts.
(Note: The looser way of connecting sentences must be re-
duced to the stricter way.)

13. If the immediate determination is not sufficient, the
meaning must be determined mediately by identity and
opposition.*

---

*To 13. In 1828 I have gradually progressed from 10.
(a) The two also include all of their secondary determinations. When something remains indefinite, it indicates
some error or omission. Care in the assumption that the
author's ideas were vague is recommended. A correct
treatment of the psychological side would be of assistance
here. (b) Passages in the same text with similar mean-
ings--the general overview should lead one to recognize
these--are to be regarded as part of the same passage. In
doing so, be careful: (α) the expressions must be related
to the unity of the entire text in the same way. Thus we
are most certain in the case of major thoughts. (β) In

136

(Note: Similarity and difference can be reduced to these two.)

    a.   Identity. Discuss the canon that "in scriptura sacra tautologia non est admittenda" [There are no tautologies in Holy Scripture.] Romans 10:9; 4:25. --I Corinthians 6:14-19; John 10:11-14, cf. 15. --Hebrews 3:1, cf. 4:14; 7:22; 8:6. I Corinthians 2:14-3:2 (John 5:31, cf. John 8:14 and Romans 3:28, cf. James 2:24, Romans 4:2 coram seo, coram nos.) --I Corinthians 3:1, cf. Hebrews 5:13. --I Corinthians 10:23, cf. John 1:15. I Corinthians 8:5; Romans 16:16, I John 5:14, 20. --John 4:24, cf. 6:63.

14. Opposition occurs in every text, but it is found most frequently in dialectical ones.*

Since this method brings almost everything in Scripture within the scope of these means of explanation, it follows that the more perfectly the interpreter attends to the whole at every point the better his work will progress.

The result of our work, then, is a complete and well-organized dictionary of Scripture. The idea of such

---

the case of secondary thoughts we are certain only when they have a quite definite sphere = treatment or when one can construe them as a whole and the relation to this whole is the same.

*On the relationship between identity and opposition. Similarity and difference is both a compound relationship and no relationship at all. It is the equivalent to the former when the degree can somehow be determined; it is almost nonexistent [null] when it is closer to an area where similar ideas [Vorstellungen] are present, because these are the least significant secondary thoughts.

a dictionary is best exemplified by that of Plato's
work. How far the New Testament dictionaries are from
this idea.

XXVIII. 15. The same rules are employed in order to discover the identities and the antitheses.
1. For no judgment can be made about a set of antitheses except by reference to a higher identity.
Likewise, and identity is recognized only by reference
to a common opposition.
2. In both cases we arrive at the certainty that we
are regarding the relationship of two statements in
the same way the author regarded it.
16. A sentence in which the same subject or predicate
governs without interruption is to be viewed as part of
the immediate context.
17. If the material which follows an interruption seems
to cohere with the basic train of thought in the text,
then it is in all probability identical with it, even
though the interruption itself may have been discontinu-
ous.
18. If the material which follows an interruption is a
secondary thought and the interruption itself a major
thought, then one can be convinced that they are identical
only by their appropriateness to the content and character
of the main train of thought.*
(Note: For this reason parables give rise to secondary
thoughts. Matthew 13.)

---

*Identity of the subject. Then discuss 18. For those
cases where the text itself is not sufficient the most
natural practice is to shift to other texts by the same
author. But not always, for although the texts may form a
unity in terms of psychological interpretation, they may
do so with respect to language only insofar as they belong
to the same genre.

19.   In dealing with leading thoughts, one can move beyond
a given text to certain other works written by that author
which may be viewed as one with the text in question.   One
may also move to the writings of others who belong to the
same school and share the same viewpoint.

20.   In dealing with secondary thoughts, the observation
noted in 18, above, relates more to an identity of the
linguistic sphere and of style than to the person and his
intention.

> (Note: To what extent can other passages containing
> the same major thoughts be used to explain secondary
> thoughts? Qualitatively, but not quantitatively;
> vague, but not suggestive.)

XXIX.   21.   The more an interpreter relies on the research
of others, the more he must be in a position to check
their judgments.

> (Note: This point ought not be discussed until later.
> --First in the section dealing with the reconstruction
> of language. For the New Testament the dogmatic ar-
> rangement is to be included.)

22.   In the application to the New Testament the philological view that considers each writing of each author
separately and the dogmatic view that considers the New
Testament as the work of a single author represent the
extremes.[20]

23.   These two views seem less far apart when one considers that the identity of the school is a factor in the
religious content and that the identity of the linguistic
sphere is a factor in the secondary thoughts.

24.   The canon established by the dogmatic point of view,
proceeding from the conviction that the Holy Spirit as a
definite personality is the author of the Scriptures, that
"one should accept a given usage as figurative only when
it is absolutely necessary" is false.[21]

XXX.   25.   The philological view contradicts its own principles when it rejects common dependency in favor of individualistic development.

26. The dogmatic point of view goes beyond its own requirements when it rejects individualistic development in
favor of dependency, and thus destroys itself.

It destroys itself because it must attribute the undeniable changes of mood and modification of view to the
Holy Spirit.

27. The question remains whether dependency or individuality should be given prominence. The philological view
must decide this question in favor of dependency.

This is so partly because the individuality of the
writers was itself a product of their relationship to
Christ and partly because special consideration is due
the more individualistic writers. (Paul is distinctive because of his dialectics, John because of his
sensitivity). But Paul was so entirely changed that
it is better to interpret him by reference to the other New Testament writings than it would be to interpret him from any pre-Christian writings of his own.
Since John evidently began to follow Christ as a young
man, he was already a Christian when his individuality
began to unfold.

28. If the philological view fails to recognize these
factors, it negates Christianity.

For if dependence on Christ was of no significance for
one's personal character and for the shortcomings of
one's upbringing, then Christ himself is of no significance.

XXXI. 29. If the dogmatic view extends the canon of the
analogy of faith beyond these limits, it negates the
Scriptures.

For a point of agreement among authors who are clear
cannot be used to clarify authors who are obscure
without explaining the scriptures on the basis of dogmatic concepts. But this would be to deny its authority and to contradict the very principles of dogmatic
interpretation. For such points of agreement are established only by a dogmatic operation which abstracts

not only from the individual characteristics of a person, about which the dogmatic view has doubts, but also from the special origin of the text, about which the dogmatic view has no doubt at all.

Every passage is an interlacing of common and distinctive traits, and so it cannot be explained correctly solely by reference to the common ones. Furthermore, the common traits cannot be correctly ascertained until every passage has been explained, and the ever-varying, relative distinction between clear and obscure passages can be carried back until originally only a single passage is clear.

30. The analogy of faith can emerge, then, only from correct interpretation, and the dogmatic canon can mean only: when no common points of agreement emerge from a group of passages that belong together, there is some error in the interpretation.[22]

Therefore, the most that can be said is that the greatest probability of misinterpretation lies with those passages which do not agree with the others.

Two class sessions are combined. The first deals with

(31). comparing the unity of the New Testament with that of the Socratic school. The other deals with

(32). distinguishing the preceeding, purely philological explanation from one that merely compiles usages.

(33). Other principles for parallelism. Essential distinction between primary and secondary passages. Possibility of identical contents with entirely different linguistic usages. For example, John and Paul, since the former is more historical and the latter more figurative.

34. It is essential to keep the two operations distinct and to be aware of which of them one is engaged in.

XXXIV. 35. If an interpreter who has the requisite linguistic knowledge must follow the same procedures used in an interpretation designed to acquire a knowledge of the language, he must mark out a definite linguistic sphere

for the range of the word by reference to parallel
passages.

All of the "authoritative" citations for word-meanings
in lexica are in fact only a collection of parallels.
36. Consequently, the old rule that "one should not look
outside of a text for a means of explanation until all of
the clues within the text have been exhausted" is considerably limited.[23]

1. For if there are words in other texts with equivalent meanings, they would be listed together in the
dictionary. The distinction between easy and difficult passages cannot be adduced in opposition to this
claim, for in fact it was this distinction that led us
to this rule.

2. The use of this old rule is especially limited
with respect to treating major thoughts. This is so
in part because a religious conversion does not alter
everything, but leaves many ideas unchanged, and in
part because some ideas current in that age were used
to combat those of the Christians.

3. In the case of secondary thoughts it is evident
that a given New Testament writer is no more closely
related to the other New Testament writers than to
anyone else with whom he shared a common circle of
thoughts, level of culture, and sphere of language.

4. This old rule is even less valuable if the Old
Testament is regarded to be part of Scripture. For
the Old Testament contains a number of confusing main
thoughts that were already alien to the New Testament
era. Moreover, its secondary thoughts arose in an age
that exerted little impact on life in New Testament
times.

37. Since meaning is not vested in the individual parts
of speech but in their connection, the closest parallels
are those in which the parts of speech have been combined
in the same way.

It is arbitrary to consider one word rather than another as the more obscure, for either could be the obscure one. Compare John 7:39 where it would be futile
to search at random among the different meanings of
πνευμα ἁγιον [Holy Spirit]. The true parallel is
Acts 19:2, and it can be argued that the real difficulty is with εἶναι [to be] which should not be here
taken strictly but means "to appear" or "to be
revealed."

XXXV. 38. Quantitative and qualitative understanding deserve equal attention.

Consequently, the interpreter should not begin solely
with the difficult passages, but should also deal with
easy ones, and with both the formal and material elements of the language, and with both words and whole
sentences.

39. The minimum of quantitative understanding is "pleonasm" [das Abundiren], the maximum is "emphasis."

1. Pleonasms occur when parts of speech do not contribute anything to the whole. But this never occurs
absolutely. Emphasis occurs when a word is to be
taken in its greatest range--an unusual circumstance--
and when it is to connote all of the secondary representations it can. These may be infinite.

2. Since the extremes of pleonasm and emphasis never
actually occur, one must begin with a middle-point
which may be taken as normal. Anything below this
mid-point may be assumed to approximate pleonasm, anything above it, emphasis.

XXXVI. 40. Pleonasms always arise for some reason,
either from a regard for the musical quality of the language or from a mechanical attraction. Unless one or the
other of these causes can be demonstrated, the language
cannot be considered "pleonastic."

1. Mechanical attraction rarely occurs except when a
combination of two parts of speech has become a formula and a cliché.

2. A pleonasm with respect to musical qualities of
language can occur only in those genres where this
musical aspect becomes predominant and in those passages where the logical element recedes, that is, when
the form of antithesis is absent.

3. In such a case parts of both the subject and the
predicate may become pleonastic. If the subject and
predicate are not contradictory, further secondary determinations of one or the other can be made.

41. Emphatic expressions are to be recognized by accented
passages and other indications.

1. The interpreter cannot unconsciously go beyond the
normal meaning of a term, and it is to be observed
that, since an emphatic use of a word is always an
abbreviation, it may be that something is inserted into the word that could just as well be placed next to
it. When such an insertion is not clear enough, the
other construction is chosen.

2. A word is emphatic only in relation to another
part of speech, and this relationship must be indicated by the way the elements are arranged.

42. The maxim that one should take as much material as
possible tautologically is as false as the maxim that as
much material as possible should be viewed emphatically.[24]

1. The former maxim is more recent. It is believed
to be justified in the interpretation of the New Testament because of its predominant form of parallelism
and its lack of logical precision. Nonetheless, this
view is wrong, and one must refer again to the discussion above. It is believed justified, especially,
whenever materials even appear to be synonymous.
XXXVII. 2. The second maxim is older, and it is related to the view that the Holy Spirit is the author
of Scripture and that the Holy Spirit does nothing in
vain. It follows, then, that nothing can be pleonastic or tautologous, but all related terms must be

emphatic. But then everything must be so regarded, for unless each passage bears the full meaning of the word, there would be something left over. But the original hearers and readers never lost sight of the personality of the author, and they were able to judge what they read and heard only by their customary way of understanding. Thus it is futile to resort to the subterfuge that the Holy Spirit had in mind the whole of inspiration-believing Christendom, which would judge according to the above maxim. Since Christendom could have originated only as a result of a correct understanding imparted to the first Christians, this maxim is completely untenable.

3. Since the truth lies somewhere in the middle, there simply is no other general rule for making judgments except that one should always keep these reservations in mind and decide which maxim can be applied least unnaturally. Especially to be mentioned here is the original justification [Urgiren] for metaphorical expressions because, used emphatically, every metaphor is a "condensed" simile. A simile, too, can be emphasized. But even these cases must be judged by the rule that the meaning of a simile must be sought from the sphere within which the simile plays. Otherwise, one ends up merely with applications and imposed meanings. Yet consider how close metaphors are to clichés, and to that extent they are not emphatic. For the most part emphasis is predominant in strictly dialectical presentations and in those marked by a high degree of wit.

XXXVIII. 43. How much of pleonastic or emphatic language is to be expected depends not only on the genre of the text but also on the degree to which the subject matter has been developed.

If the content of some sphere of ideas has already been thoroughly developed, one can begin with a representative selection, and the type of discourse will

determine when and where emphatic or pleonastic language is to be expected. But if the content is so new
that language for it has not yet developed, it becomes
somewhat uncertain whether the phraseology selected
for treating it is effective. When the language is to
designate a very clear point, the author is inclined
to clarify ambiguous expressions by adding others.
This results in prolix expressions that are sometimes
mistaken for tautologies or for emphases. But the
truth is that such expressions ought not be regarded
either as identical or as antithetical, but as units
from which the idea should be grasped by considering
both together. In the New Testament this is the case
with Paul, at least, because his terminology depends
so heavily on oral tradition. In John there is very
little of this. False emphasis has led people to join
various expressions (renewal, illumination, rebirth)
into a dogmatic system of concepts, and that practice
has resulted in a confusing, unscientific excess.[25]
False tautologies have led people to assume only a
minimum of content in expressions, and so to give up
the concept itself.

44. Quantitative understanding of statements consists in
standing the parts of speech and how they have been connected.

Statements are related both to each other and to the
unity of the discourse. In the latter case the key
consideration is to distinguish between the major and
secondary thoughts; in the former case the key is to
differentiate between coordinating and subordinating
relations. A major thought is a statement made for
its own sake. A secondary thought is a statement made
to explain something, even though it may be far more
detailed than a major thought. Major thoughts are
recognized by the concepts which they contain. Since
secondary thoughts are superfluous and have no place
in the ideal of a strictly scientific discourse, the

relationship between major and secondary thoughts
should be judged in the same way pleonasm and emphasis
are judged.

Whether statements are coordinate or subordinate must
be decided on the basis of the connective terms and
the way in which they are combined. Nonetheless, attention to the contents may aid in this decision. The
more definite the forms for combining thoughts in a
given type of discourse, the less necessary it becomes
to consider the contents. And vice versa, the more
clear the context, the less puzzling are the usages of
the forms of combination become.

In loose forms of combination such as we find throughout the New Testament, it is difficult to distinguish
the major and secondary thoughts by referring to the
linguistic sphere because the distinction is not sharp
enough and because the interrelationship of the materials allows each to cross over and become the other.
In such cases attention must be paid to the contents,
and by determing how the sentences relate to each
other, one must then find how they relate to the
whole.

(Note: This account helps explain how many passages
have been classified, improperly, as dogmatic. This
incorrect classification is due to the maxim that all
of the dogmatic passages in the New Testament must be
major thoughts. This maxim is untenable.)

Concluding Remark

The topics we have just discussed have led us to technical
interpretation. This does not mean that the maxim, each
task must be self-sufficient, is untrue, but the comprehensive knowledge of language that it presupposes cannot
be reached except by interpretation itself.

If my knowledge of language is incomplete, I must, of
course, turn to others for help. But since I can make use
of such aid only with my faulty knowledge of language,

technical interpretation must always supplement grammatical interpretation. The reverse is also true. I can make use of the knowledge others have of an author only by means of my faulty knowledge of them. Therefore, grammatical interpretation must supplement technical interpretation.

Part 2: Technical Interpretation

1. Both technical and grammatical interpretation begin with a general overview of a text designed to grasp its unity and the major features of its composition. But in technical interpretation the unity of the work, its theme, is viewed as the dynamic principle impelling the author, and the basic features of the composition are viewed as his distinctive nature, revealing itself in that movement.
(Note: Unity of the work. --Its organization is often merely external and vague. Can be destroyed. At other times the organization is deliberately obscured. The more unified the work, the more artistic it is, and vice versa. The artistic quality of a work is not to be judged solely by its language, for example, in dialogues and letters. --Extremely loose and extremely tight writing are outside the scope of interpretation. --Preliminary task: to know in advance the aim of a work, its circle, and its ideas.)
The unity of the work is to be found in the way the sphere of language has been grammatically constructed. The chief features of composition are to be found in the way the connections between the thoughts have been constructed. Technical interpretation attempts to identify what has moved the author to communicate. Objective differences, such as whether the treatment is popular or scientific, are functions of this motivating principle. Nonetheless, an author organizes his thought in his own peculiar way, and this peculiar way is reflected in the arrangement he chooses. Likewise, an author always has secondary ideas which are

determined by his special character. Thus the distinctiveness of an author may be recognized by the secondary ideas that distinguish him from others.

To recognize an author in this way is to recognize him as he has worked with language. To some extent he initiates something new in the language by combining subjects and predicates in new ways. Yet to some extent he merely repeats and transmits the language he has received. Likewise, when I know his language, I recognize how the author is a product of the language and stands under its potency. These two views, then, are only two ways of looking at the same thing.

2. The ultimate goal of technical interpretation is nothing other than a development of the beginning, that is, to consider the whole of the author's work in terms of its parts and in every part to consider the content as what moved the author and the form as his nature moved by that content.

When I have exhausted the meaning of every part of the text, there is nothing left to be understood. Moreover, it is self-evident that the relative distinction between understanding the parts and understanding the whole is mediated by the fact that each part is to be treated in the same way as the whole. The aim, however, can be achieved only by holding these two considerations together. Although much of a text can be understood by grammatical interpretation alone, grammatical interpretation cannot grasp how the work is a necessary undertaking of the author, since a sense for this necessity emerges only if the genesis of the text is never lost from view.

3. The goal of technical interpretation should be formulated as the complete understanding of style.

We are accustomed to restrict the term "style" to the way language is handled. But thoughts and language are intertwined, and an author's distinctive way of

treating the subject is manifested by his organization
of his material and by his use of language.

Since a person always has numerous ideas, the development of any specific one involves accepting som-
thing and excluding something else. --Yet when an
idea does not develop from the distinctive character
of the author, but is acquired by study or by custom,
or is cultivated for its effect, then there is mannerism, and mannerism is always poor style.

4. The goal of technical interpretation can only be approximated.

Despite all our progress we are still far from the
goal. There are still conflicts over Homer, and the
three tragedians still cannot be perfectly distinguished.[26] --Not only do we never understand an individual view [Anschauung] exhaustively, but what we do
understand is always subject to correction. This becomes evident when we consider that, beyond doubt, the
best test is the attempt to imitate an author. But
since imitation is so rarely successful and since
higher criticism is still embroiled in disputes, we
know we are quite far from our goal.

5. Before technical interpretation can begin, one must
learn the way the author received his subject matter and
the language, and whatever else can be known about the
author's distinctive manner [Art und Weise] of writing.

This first task includes learning about the state of a
given genre when the author began to write. The second includes learning about the use of language current in this area and related areas. Consequently,
exact understanding in this regard requires knowing
about related literature current in that era as well
as earlier models of style. In technical interpretation there is no substitute for such comprehensive and
systematic research.

Learning about the author's manner of writing is a
laborious task, and the easiest way to gain such

knowledge is to turn to secondary sources. These
works, however, make judgments which must be assessed
by acts of interpretation. Consequently, reliance on
such distant works is to be avoided. As aids for
understanding, biographical sketches of authors were
originally included in editions of their works, but
they usually neglected discussing the question of literary models. Certainly a useful prolegomenon will
give the most necessary information about the other
two points.

On the basis of this background knowledge and the initial overview of the work, the interpreter develops a
provisional conception in terms of which the distinctiveness of the author is to be sought.

6. From the moment it begins, technical interpretation
involves two methods: a divinatory and a comparative.
Since each method refers back to the other, the two should
never be separated.

By leading the interpreter to transform himself, so to
speak, into the author, the divinatory method seeks to
gain an immediate comprehension of the author as an
individual. The comparative method proceeds by sub-
suming the author under a general type. It then tries
to find his distinctive traits by comparing him with
the others of the same general type. Divinatory
knowledge is the feminine strength in knowing people;
comparative knowledge, the masculine.

Each method refers back to the other. The divinatory
is based on the assumption that each person is not only a unique individual in his own right, but that he
has a receptivity to the uniqueness of every other
person.

This assumption in turn seems to presuppose that each
person contains a minimum of everyone else, and so
divination is aroused by comparison with oneself. But
how is it possible for the comparative method to subsume a person under a general type? Obviously, either

by another act of comparison (and this continues into infinity) or by divination.

The two methods should never be separated. Divination becomes certain only when it is corroborated by comparisons. Without this confirmation, it always tends to be fanatical. But comparison does not provide a distinctive unity. The general and the particular must interpenetrate, and only divination allows this to happen.

7. The idea of the work, as the will which leads to the actual composition, can be understood only by the joint consideration of two factors: the content of the text and its range of effects.

The content itself does not dictate how it must be treated. As a rule the theme of the work is easy to identify, even if it is not explicitly stated. But for that very reason we can be misled. --What is usually called the "aim" of the work in the strict sense of the word is a different matter entirely. It is often quite external, and it exercises only a limited influence on a few passages. This influence can usually be accounted for from the character of the people who were being addressed. But if one knows who these people were and what effect these passages were to have on them, then, since these factors determine the composition of the work, the interpreter knows everything that is necessary.

MANUSCRIPT 3'

A DRAFT FOR THE PRESENTATION

OF THE SECOND PART[27]

Monday, Sept. 2

General Survey

I. By a knowledge of the individuality of an author,
grammatical interpretation can be brought to a level that
it could not reach on its own.

II. The goal is to reproduce the subjective bases for the
combination of particular elements of a text in order to
learn how to grasp the train of thought. (Note: Ordinarily, little is written about this part of interpretation,
except with respect to its subsidiary first use. The result is only partial understanding.)

To I. By this means attention is directed to (a) qualitative, false understanding, (b) quantitative, understanding too much and too little.

> To a. In this case grammatical interpretation has
> hegemony and technical interpretation helps only where
> grammatical interpretation is ambiguous or where the
> conditions for its application are missing. This lies
> in the natural relationship of the author to the lan-
> guage.
>
> To b. Grammatical interpretation alone cannot avoid
> quantitative misunderstanding. In dealing with allu-
> sions, for example, it depends on immediate under-
> standing and considers anything that is not grammati-
> cally necessary to be arbitrary, thus overlooking the

references to the correct meaning. (Note: Thus a subsidiary usage again becomes autocratic and the opposition is dissolved.) Searching for too much meaning is due to false application of the distinctiveness of an author or from an incorrect grasp of that distinctiveness.

To II. This procedure includes consideration of (a) the objective train of thought, including everything that expresses the author's immediate relation to the subject matter of the work and all of the elements essential to the composition; (b) the subjective train of thought, the secondary representations: (α) determining the field from which the author draws the secondary representations, (β) accounting for their appearance in certain places. Both (1) from the totality of his personality and (2) from the relations between those which he had in mind. (Note: The above leads us back again to the objective train of thought, for it has an influence on the application of the train of thought.)

Tuesday, September 3

I. On Discovering and Reproducing the Objective Train of Thought.

(Note: One must begin with this task because it is at this point that it begins to be of assistance to grammatical interpretation.)

Elucidation

1. The maximum extent of such reproduction is imitation--to be able to write on a given subject in the same way as another would have treated it. Poor imitations are only copies of a particular member of the main antitheses, and, indeed, mainly of the external members.

An imitator of the use of language rather than of the composition, of the subjective train of thought more than the objective. Just as a copy is perfect only when it reproduces the identity present within this antithesis, so too one's knowledge is complete only when one recognizes the identity present in the opposition.

2.   This identity must be found in a threefold combination: (a) the principle governing the coherence of the leading thoughts; (b) the principle governing the coherence of the secondary thoughts; (c) the principle governing the coherence of the leading thoughts and the secondary thoughts and their interrelations.

Corollaries.

1.   The first task, then, is to distinguish between the objective and subjective thoughts. 2.   Therefore, technical interpretation has difficulty with authors in whom this distinction is hard to make. Note: These difficult authors are neither the most profound nor the most shallow, but those who are confused. 3.   The coherence of the leading ideas is recognized along with the author's peculiar view of the subject matter of the work. The coherence of the secondary representations is to be recognized from the relationship between the author's ability to use ideas and the subject matter of the work--with the interest he had in one thing or another, especially during the preparation of the work, and therefore with the entire relation of his personality to the work. Consequently, it is especially important to trace, in addition to the actual train of thought, the sequence of the leading and secondary ideas as they are interwoven.

Wednesday, September 4

1.   General requirements for the transition from leading to secondary thoughts.

1.   There is no occasion for secondary representations to follow a clearly and completely expressed leading thought because there is no necessity or stimulus to do so. Rather there is a stimulus to use the clear insight that has emerged along with the thought as a continuation of it. (Note: Thus, when such a presentation is followed by material not in continuity with

it, this material is not to be taken as a secondary
idea, but as a preparation for the next leading
thought.) Exceptions occur (a) where the presentation
of the leading idea is disjointed and must be gleaned
from the details, partly because it has degenerated
into secondary ideas and partly because it has occasioned them; (b) where one detects in the presentation
that the author had extracted himself somewhat from
the dominant subject and yielded to a free train of
thought. For in such cases he will also yield to secondary ideas which arise.

2. Return to the objective train of thought. Two
types: (a) a return to the leading thoughts with which
one began; (b) an advance to a new leading thought.
--If a secondary idea is part of a group of elaborations, the return may be cut off entirely. A transition through diversity is always artistic and must be
interpreted from a broader context. Throughout the
process one should sense what will follow.

2. General Characteristics of the Contents.

1. The leading thoughts. (a) The contents of the
leading thoughts are given in the idea of the work,
including the peculiar viewpoint of the author, and
its theme. (b) One must also consider the range of
the secondary ideas and the taste of the author in
order to determine the range and complexity of the
leading thoughts, since the relationship depends on
the author's taste.

2. Even if the author's personality is known in its
entirety, the secondary ideas can never be discovered
at the beginning merely from the author's principle
of selection and method. The author himself did not
have them in mind at that time; rather, they were
aroused in him in the course of his work. The task is
too complicated even when one tries "to understand the
author better than he understood himself."[28] Thus
"divination" can extend only to what is nearest at

hand. Since they consist of two elements, knowledge and personal relationships, one must learn from the character of the author how each was related to the subject matter of the work and where emphasis on the one or the other can be anticipated. Note: Divination is far more common in ordinary life than it is in the study of texts, and yet in some respects it is more difficult in the former than the latter.

2. Consideration of particular relationships.[29]

A. One must distinguish simple secondary ideas used for elucidating and enlivening an idea for which others could have been substituted from allusions which an author relies upon to achieve a special secondary purpose.

> (Note: 1. Allusions are so named because they involve a double reference: one that warrants the use of the term in the context and a second that is to attain a secondary aim that lies outside of the context.
> 2. This secondary aim may relate to other parts of the presentation which are to be completed or prepared for by aid of something in addition to and outside of the series of main ideas or they may relate to the external relationships of the author.)

The relationship is entirely different when the secondary ideas arise merely from a need or stimulus of the moment and when they are viewed as a special task. In the former case an artistic application is necessary, but one in which the sense [Sinn] of the idea [Vorstellung] is to be recognized.

Corollaries. This relationship generally occurs
> 1. in the many authors who always let their personality come into prominence, and
> 2. in the presentation of a topic which is inseparable from its external relationships, and

3. in circumstances where the author is restricted such that not everything can be stated
straightforwardly.

Thursday, September 5

b. The interpreter must distinguish between the character of a pure presentation and that of an occasion-
alistic effusion, between major works and occasional
writings, between objective and popular writings. Influence on the train of thought.

1. Occasional writings--greater relationship of
secondary ideas, a sphere comprised of special
connections about which often nothing can be
learned. But, on the other hand, they are more
uniform because they always relate to the occasional interest. Objective writings--narrower relationship, but scattered throughout the entire
mass of ideas and items of knowledge.

2. In objective writings the leading thoughts are
organized in accordance with the author's special
point of view. In occasional writings they are
organized not only in accord with the nature of
the subject matter, but also in terms of the interest of the moment, and the organization of the
piece results from the conflict between these two
factors. (Note: Texts in which the occasional interest, because of this "unification" [Eignung],
is not sufficiently dominant to mediate the conflict, to do full justice to the occasional interest from the very start and in this way to represent the whole as the product of a mechanical
succession.)

Corollary. By following these rules the interpreter
comes to note three other factors: the material that
follows, the coloring of the leading thoughts, and the
immediate sequence of ideas. But the two processes
must always be kept together. Otherwise, the interpreter will not do justice to the goal of total under-

standing because of his preoccupation with the richness of detail, or, because of the details, he will fail to give the coherence of the whole the value it deserves.

Friday, September 6

Application to the New Testament.

1. In certain instances imitation is easy here, too. John's fragmentary style of writing, Paul's entangled sentences. But the character of the author rests in the unity of these external traits with internal traits, and with the material external traits.

2. There is only one confused author who gave no coloring to his leading ideas and whose work, therefore, contains certain points which are difficult to clarify. That author is Peter. He always remains somewhat removed from the power of his subject matter.

3. Application to the leading thoughts. (Note: The task of making them into images. Distinguishing between historical and didactic, and between free and didactic passages.) Here, again, John and Paul are at opposite extremes. Paul develops his ideas more discursively, and so the entire train of thought must be comprehended as a unity. John tends to dwell on a single idea and so puts particular motifs side by side.

4. All of them draw from the same sphere of secondary ideas: (a) personal relationships between the writer and reader to whom the ideas were directed; (b) range of thought, literature, and history by which the ideas were explicated.

Different authors related these two elements differently. Paul and Matthew are more similar to each other than either is to John. John's gospel exhibits a more personal relationship to Christ. In the First Epistle the relationship is more reserved. Wherever Paul dealt with personality he regarded it as a leading idea.

MANUSCRIPT 4

THE SEPARATE EXPOSITION OF THE

SECOND PART (1826-27)

Part 2: On Technical Interpretation

I.

Introduction. Parallels to grammatical interpretation.
Grammatical interpretation. To understand the discourse
and how it has been composed in terms of its language.
Technical interpretation: To understand the discourse as a
presentation of thought. Composed by a human being and so
understood in terms of a human being.
Grammatical interpretation. The person and his activity
disappear and seem to be merely an organ of the language.
Technical interpretation: The language and its determining
power disappear and seem to be merely an organ of the person, in the service of his individuality, just as in grammatical interpretation the personality is in the service
of the language.
Grammatical interpretation. Not possible without technical interpretation. Technical interpretation: not possible without grammatical interpretation. For how shall I
know a person except from his discourse, specifically,
from this text before me?
Grammatical interpretation. Viewed in isolation, the
ideal is to understand in complete abstraction from technical interpretation. Likewise, in technical interpretation the ideal would be to understand in complete abstraction from grammatical interpretation.

161

Explanation. To be specific: (1) Our knowledge of the author already leads us to anticipate a particular style,
even apart from a consideration of the language. He could
have written in another language. (2) The connections and
contents, which are the proper objects of grammatical interpretation, are understood solely on the basis of the
way people construct their statements.
Grammatical interpretation. Understanding is gained by
seeing how all of the parts cohere. Technical interpretation: Reconstructing the overall coherence of the text is
not complete until all of the details are treated.
Grammatical interpretation is divided into two contrasting
tasks. So is technical interpretation. The first task is
to discover the individuality of an author, and the other
is to recognize with definiteness how this individuality
is expressed.
Grammatical interpretation. The one task is to regard the
text as a unity, that is, as a general view [Anschauung];
the other is to regard it in its particularity, that is,
as personally delimited. Likewise, in technical interpretation the unity is the general view present in an author's total literary output, and the particularity is the
delimited application of this unity to specific topics.
Grammatical interpretation. Each task presupposes the
other. The same is true in technical interpretation. For
how can one gain the general view [Anschauung] except by
joining together several partial views? Therefore, these
particulars must have already been understood, and how
could their contents be understood except in terms of the
general unity.
Grammatical interpretation. It is directed toward lan-
guage--not toward language as a general concept or as an
aggregate of discrete units, but toward the nature of a
particular language. Technical interpretation: It is directed toward the possible ways of combining and expressing thoughts--not as a general concept, as logical laws,

or as an empirical aggregate, but as a function of the
nature of the individual person.

Explanation.

1. When a language is regarded as a general concept,
nothing remains but the necessary forms for subject
and predicate and syntax. These structures cannot
serve as a positive but only as a negative means for
explanation, because what contradicts them cannot be
understood at all. The same situation arises when the
ability to think is regarded as a general concept or
as logical laws. Then anything that contradicts them
cannot be regarded as thinking at all. But the capacity to think cannot be understood merely in terms of
the concept itself.

2. A collection of observations about a language is
not a means for explanation but the result of previous
explanations which can be augmented by further study.
This holds true for technical interpretation, too.
Observations about the power to combine thoughts or
about psychological laws are at best suggestions that
call attention to something that contradicts them or
to something special and unique.

Grammatical interpretation. The distinctive nature of a
language is the specific modification of its view of the
world [Anschauung]. Technical interpretation: Character,
the individual nature of an author, is a specific modification of the ability to think. Organic with nature.
Each plant carries out a special modification of pre-
established processes.

II.

Grammatical interpretation. The individuality of a people's language is connected to the individuality manifest
in all of its other common activities. But we are not
concerned with this connection and its common center.
Technical interpreation: The individuality manifest in a
person's way of combining and presenting thoughts is connected with every other expression of his individuality.

Consequently, the more precisely an interpreter knows any one of these expressions, the more similarity he discovers with the others. Again, we do not deal with this connection and its mid-point, but only with the peculiarity of the presentation = style. Explanation of what is necessary for all arts, and so for style as well.

Grammatical interpretation. The elements of a language, as presentations of a specially modified capacity for viewing the world [Anschauungsvermögens], cannot be construed a priori, but can be known only by comparing numerous individual cases. Likewise, in technical interpretation the various individualities cannot be construed a priori.

In grammatical interpretation individuality cannot be grasped by a concept. Individuality must be intuited. Similarly, in technical interpretation, a concept cannot be derived from an author's style.

In grammatical interpretation to understand a language completely would be to understand its center. In technical interpretation style is understood only by a fully complete knowledge of an author's character. In both cases the goal can never be reached, but only approximated.

The fact that grammatical interpretation presupposes technical interpretation does not make it impossible, but only gives it more precise determination. The same holds for technical interpretation. Certain expressions are easier (i.e., easier in that they do not require technical interpretation, but are understandable purely in terms of grammatical interpretation). These provide the first general insight into the individuality, and in turn this insight makes the more difficult expressions understandable, thereby improving on the interpreter's initial grasp of the individuality, and so on into infinity.

It could be objected that anything understandable in grammatical terms alone could hardly provide insight into individuality, for although it can be understood grammati-

cally, its necessity cannot be grasped. It could have
been stated in several other ways. Therefore, the meaning
of such passages is to be determined on the basis of their
individuality, which can be more precisely specified by a
"transition" to technical interpretation. The claim that
grammatical interpretation itself requires technical interpretation applies only to an interpreter's initial
grasp of the coherence of the text, which precedes understanding each part. This makes the operation possible
and raises it to the level of art.
Even granting such individuality, it could be objected
that it does not apply in a given case.

1. Not every author has it--certainly not. In some
cases, however, entire classes represent one individuality, and the members of the class serve merely as
organs or as particular expressions of the class.

2. Individuality rests more in the subject matter or
in the artistic form than in the author, for example,
historical style differs from philosophical. Note.
The most important task is to recognize every art form
by its author's style, and that is done by becoming
better acquainted with the author. Thus it can be
known quite well how Plato, for example, would have
written had he written history. The distinctiveness
of an author's style, then, is evident throughout a
variety of forms.

III.

This claim may be further clarified. When an author man-
ifests in various forms of work certain traits that are
contrary to his own character, we cannot take these traits
as indicative of the individuality of his style. Instead,
we designate them by a term of reproach, "mannerism." The
individuality of an author's style may be modified in the
various genres, yet it remains the same. Moreover, when
an author incorporates traits distinctive to another work
into his own product which is similar in form, we can recognize them as inauthentic because there are conspicuous

embellishments that would not be found in a work of that
form. This is the origin of all florid style, <u>flos ora-</u>
<u>tionis</u>. It could perhaps be demonstrated that the an-
cient's view that an author's individuality must coincide
with a single, specific form was due to the fact that authors never ventured beyond a single form. But against
this claim we can cite the contemporary expectation that
an author must work in several forms and the assumption
that only an inferior talent would limit himself to a single form. The basis of the distinction is now clear. The
ancients emphasized national character more strongly. For
this reason ancient authors adhered to those forms which
preserved this character, and they used these forms as
models of perfection which were to be imitated. In our
day, however, individuality is supposed to stand out and
be evident. Therefore, our authors try to accentuate
their individuality by various means and they give up trying for mechanical perfection.
Thus individual unity remains the most important consideration, and all other matters must be found in terms of it.

Discovering the Unity of Style

Law. Each author has his own style. The only exceptions
are those who have no individuality at all, but these as a
whole can be grouped together.
Determination. Since this unity cannot be grasped concep-
tually but only intuitively, at first only its outlines
can be determined. They are: distinctiveness of the composition, beginning with the overall organization of the
text and continuing to the particular way of handling language as the final clue for "discovering" the author's individuality.
Explanation.

  1. By its very nature the hermeneutical operation
      dictates that the interpreter begin by considering the
      overall organization of the work. Hermeneutics must
      begin with an overview of the whole. This first step

is frequently omitted, as interpreters start off by considering the author's peculiar way of using language. But judgments about an author's personal use of language are completely unreliable if they are not in harmony with the composition, and too often they are preoccupied with minutiae.

2. These two goals together constitute the whole task. Style refers to both the composition and the treatment of language.

3. These two elements are not to be viewed as absolute opposites. Thoughts which are properly elements of the composition are also parts of the means of presentation, that is, actual language; and, vice versa, language often becomes the essential element of composition.

IV.

Two methods. Comparing the text with others, and considering it in and for itself. The comparative method is regarded the better way, but even so it is not necessary for works on physiognomy and the like. In order to identify those parts that correspond to parts in other works, this method must break up the whole, and so it is worthless. (Nota bene: One should begin with the method that considers the text in and for itself.) The comparative method should be employed only to direct attention to those elements which most clearly indicate an author's individuality. In applying this method, however, these elements should be compared to the whole rather than to other elements, because each element is an index to the principle by which an author's individuality is expressed. (Note. Considering what an author has excluded plays a role in this procedure.) Therefore, to explain how an author forms language, one should make comparisons with the entire sphere of the language; to explain how an author composed the work, one should make comparisons with the complete range of the theme.

1. Discovering the individuality of the composition.
The process is as follows: The unity of the whole is
grasped and then seen in its relation to the various sections within the whole. The first task shows the author's
idea to be the basis for the composition. The latter task
shows his actual way of grasping and presenting it. The
author's idea vouches only for his merit, not for his individuality. But certainly the way in which he presents
his idea vouches for his individuality, for it depends on
the distinctive way he organizes his view of the topic.
Once an overall view of the work has been gained, this
view is applied to the details. The degree of harmony between the general view and the details determined the literary merit of the author. In this process the interpreter's initial insight into the author's individuality is
confirmed or corrected, and as the process continues, this
insight becomes more exact.

First task: Finding the inner unity or the theme of the
work.
Note:
    1. It is customary to call this inner unity the "pur-
    pose" of the work, but this is wrong. The more arbi-
    trary the production of the work, the greater the dif-
    ference between its idea and purpose. In comparison
    to the idea, the purpose may be quite subordinate, and
    as soon as the idea and the purpose are equated, the
    purpose seems to serve only as a means.
    2. It is normally supposed that the most direct way
    to find the inner unity of the work is to examine the
    author's own statements at the beginning or at the
    end. This is wrong. In many writings what the author
    declares to be his subject matter is in fact quite
    subordinate to the actual theme. More frequently
    still the purpose is equated with the idea of the
    work. Examples of the former error are available in
    modern literature; examples of the latter may be found

even in ancient literature. In epic literature the
declarations refer only to the purpose, not to the
idea.
Resolution.
    1. Compare the relationship between the beginning and
the end of a work. (Note. Therefore, the first overview of the work begins in as elementary a way as possible.) A developing relationship is characteristic
of historical and rhetorical compositions. A static
relationship is characteristic of intuitive compositions. A cyclical relationship is characteristic of
dialectical compositions.
V.

Cautions. [1] For both the beginning and the end one
can of course distinguish between what is related to
the purpose and what to the idea. [2] One can also
determine the true beginning and the true end.
(a) The whole begins at the beginning of its first
part and ends at the conclusion of its last part. Example. It could easily be supposed that the ending of
John represents the conclusion to the final section,
but its identity of style with the beginning shows
that it is the conclusion to the entire text. (b) One
should identify the boundaries of the whole. The
failure to do this has led to real follies in poetics,
as when the Iliad, or the Pentateuch, or Joshua have
been viewed as originally whole. Likewise, however,
unified a book may be, it can consist of many wholes
which must be separated from one another.[1]
    2. If the beginning and end do not provide any, or
insufficient, information to establish the unity, one
should consider the accentuated passages. Passages
which have been given equal emphasis must relate to
the idea of the work in the same way, and so they follow from the idea. (Note: Here again it is evident
that grammatical interpretation is employed in order
to identify the accentuated passages. Moreover, gram-

matical interpretation is necessary for the other task
of technical interpretation, that is, for determining
the distinctive use of language of an individual. For
each person has his own way of accentuating points.)
Corollary.

(1) In some compositions no passages are accentuated. But in such cases the above holds in a negative way because one discovers with each presupposition that it must have been accentuated in one
way or another. Accentuated passages are absent:
(a) in works that approximate an epic structure
where, as in an immediate sense intuition, nothing
may stand out; (b) in works with a certain noble
simplicity, above all in practical works; and
(c) in works marked by dry wit and irony.

(2) In some works there are passages which were
falsely accentuated in a deliberate way, as in
persiflage. Dictionaries are available to us, but
they are the least likely sources for identifying
such passages. But a particular accent given a
passage can be of special assistance in going beyond the apparent seriousness of the subject matter.

3. One should then press further, tracing the emphases and subordinate elements of each part, until one
reaches as it were a point of rest that forms the immediate context. The more exactly the diminution of
accent corresponds to its distance from the presupposed idea, the more the presupposition is confirmed.
At the same time, the more the degree of emphasis dev-
iates from and clashes with the presupposed idea, the
more suspect the presupposition. Corollary. Nevertheless, one should not add a second hypothesis, for
that would presuppose an imperfection in the author,
i.e., that he was not always equally clear in his
awareness of his idea but allowed himself to drift off

into other matters. Yet one should give constant attention to this possibility.

Second Task: Discovering the individuality of the composition.
Explanation. This is the first truly subjective aspect. An author can convey individuality by means of several totally different ideas. Or, in writing about the same idea, two different authors will express completely different individual characteristics.
Solution.
    1. There are two ways: immediate intuition [<u>Anschauung</u>] and comparison with other works. (Neither way is self-sufficient.) Immediate intuition cannot be communicated; comparison never quite reaches the true individuality. The two ways must be combined by relating them to the totality of possibilities.
    2. The interpreter must seek to discover this totality of possibilities, and this is done only by comparing a given text with others. It may then be seen how, within this totality, the major parts of the work which need to be explained belong together. The individuality is to be grasped from this correlation between the whole and the parts.
Explanation.
    1. The preliminary task is to find all of the possibilities available to the author. Therefore, the interpreter must remain within the boundaries of nature and of the era. (Those places where the author himself creatively altered these boundaries are evident). The individuality of the nation and of the era form the bases for an author's individuality. For example, it should not be assumed that compositions characteristic of our age or the sentimentality of our lyric poets were available to ancient authors. (Note: Therefore, an author is to be understood in terms of his own age.)

2. This totality of possibilities is found (a) by
comparing a given work with works of contemporaneous
authors and with similar works; and (b) by referring
to similarities between a given work and others of
different types, as well as to works from other eras,
but always in accord with universal laws of combination. For example, were the work of only one Hebrew
historian extant, we could still construct the totality from the lyrical poets.

3. In the actual application of the procedure these
two aspects, comparison and intuition, may be given
varying weight, sometimes with emphasis given to comparison of particulars and at other times with emphasis given to immediate intuition. Specify the conditions under which this is done.

Result. As a unity, individuality cannot be reproduced.
It always remains indescribable, and can be characterized
only as harmony. The main points to be considered are the
following.

1. The distinctive manner in which an author formu-
lates his ideas, his material literary intention
[Gesinnung], is recognized by the way he selects and
arranges his material. An author's inclination toward
austerity or grace in his composition, his formal literary intention, is recognized by the way he relates
the details of his work in the overall plan.

2. The inclination toward austerity or elegance of
composition, the author's formal literary intention,
is recognized by how the added material relates to the
whole through the coherence of the details. Note.
Most consider this trait to be a function of the individuality of the era. This view is tenable only insofar as poverty [Mangel] is the cause of the austerity
or luxury and effeminacy are the causes of the elegance. Examples show that contemporaneous authors
differ widely in this respect.

3. Digressions from the actual objective train of
thought may be due to the influence of ideas arising
from the author's state of mind, or to the reader's
train of thought, or to the popular character of the
work. [Note.[2] Many consider the presence of digressions to be characteristic of a certain genre, but digressions occur in every genre. Of course, the interpreter must consider to what extent the subject matter
of the work occasions the author to think of a particular audience. The distinction between the way materials are arranged in works and occasional writings is
the best illustration of this point. Sometimes these
organizational schemes are quite detailed. These are
not, however, inferior types of literature. Plato and
Lessing wrote nothing but occasional pieces. [There
was a time in German literature when it was considered
presumptuous to write anything else], but now every
fool wants to write a book. The inclination to write
one or the other, then, depends on the person's character.

Application to the New Testament.

THE ACADEMY ADDRESSES OF 1829: ON THE CONCEPT OF

HERMENEUTICS, WITH REFERENCE TO F. A. WOLF'S

INSTRUCTIONS AND AST'S TEXTBOOK

The First Address

Read on August 12, 1829.[1]

Many, perhaps most, of the activities which make up
human life may be carried out at one of three levels. One
level is almost spiritless and entirely mechanical; the
second is based on a wealth of experiences and observations; and the third is artistic in the true sense of the
term. It seems to me that interpretation, too, is marked
by these three levels, at least insofar as the word "interpretation" refers to understanding all foreign or
strange speech. The first and lowest level we encounter
daily, in the market place and in the streets as well as
in many circles of society, wherever people converse about
common topics in such a way that the speaker always knows
almost immediately and with certainty what the other will
respond, and language is tossed back and forth as a ball.
Most of the time we seem to operate at the second level.
This sort of interpretation is practiced in our schools
and universities and in the commentaries of philologians
and theologians, the two groups who have worked this field
most extensively. The treasure of instructive observations and references found in their works adequately at-
tests that many of them are true artists of interpretation. Even so, juxtaposed to this wealth of information

we often find instances where difficult passages are given
wild and arbitrary explanations and where some of the most
beautiful passages are carelessly overlooked or foolishly
distorted because of the interpreter's pedantic lack of
sensitivity. But when a person who is not himself profi-
cient in such matters is called upon to interpret, he
needs, in addition to these treasures, a primer with a
solid methodology that not only presents the fruits of
masterful studies but also presents in reputable scientific form the total range and foundations of the method.
This is all the more necessary when that person is supposed to introduce inquisitive youth to the art of interpretation and to direct them in it. Consequently, for my
own sake as well as for that of my audience, when I began
to lecture on hermeneutics I searched for the best treatment of the method. But my search was in vain. Neither
the numerous theological compendia--though many of them,
such as Ernesti's book, are considered products of sound
philological study--nor even the few purely philological
essays on interpretation offered more than compilations of
individual rules extracted from the researches of the
masters.[2] Moreover, although these rules were sometimes
clear, frequently they were quite ambiguous; and although
they were now and again arranged in a helpful fashion, at
other times the arrangement was unsatisfactory. I had
high expectations when Fülleborn's philological encyclopedia, based on Wolf's lectures, was published.[3] But the
few references to hermeneutics in it did not amount even
to a sketch of a general hermeneutical theory. And since
this work was directed specifically to the literature of
classical antiquity, just as most handbooks are designed
specifically for the study of the Holy Scriptures, I found
myself no more content than before.

The essays mentioned in the title of this address
are the most significant ones to appear since that time.
Because Wolf is one of the best minds among us, and one of
our most independent and creative philologians, and

because Ast is trying to develop a philosophically-oriented philology, it would seem all the more instructive and useful to combine the strengths of both. Thus I thought it appropriate to follow their lead and to relate my own ideas about the task of interpretation to theirs.

Wolf intentionally avoids structuring his essay in a systematic form. This may be because he always takes care to avoid even the slightest hint of pedantry, preferring to leave to others the laborious and rather banal task of putting together the remarks he strews about so gracefully and elegantly, or it may be because he does not consider such a structure suitable for a lead article in a general journal that advances no systematic position of its own.[4] Ast, in contrast, considers a systematic form essential, and at the outset he asserts that no theory can be communicated scientifically without philosophical support.[5] Nonetheless, since Wolf assures us that he intended the contents of his essay to serve as an introduction for a philological encyclopedia, we may assume that he had thought through his statements with this purpose in mind, and we are justified in believing that his own theory is contained in this essay.[6]

Wolf puts together grammar, hermeneutics, and criticism as preparatory studies that provide entry to the philological disciplines per se, as the organon of the science of antiquity.[7] Ast, however, attempts to treat these same three disciplines as an appendix to his as yet unpublished outline of philology.[8] The two men are not so far apart. Even Ast's view, although he is not very clear about how the appendix is related to the main work, certainly means that his exposition of philology has led him to see the necessity of treating all three disciplines scientifically. No one would dare to deny that grammar, criticism, and hermeneutics are closely related, as these men maintain. But I would like to focus on hermeneutics, leaving the other two aside for the moment.

Certainly the works of classical antiquity, as
masterpieces of human language, are the most excellent and
worthy subjects with which the art of interpretation normally has to deal. But it is undeniable, too, that many
scholars have worked on other texts with great success,
especially on the Christian Bible, which is not such a
rich source for philologians. Were an encyclopedia for
the study of these texts to be constructed, then without
question hermeneutics, along with several other preparatory studies, would constitute an organon for Christian
theology.[9] If, then, hermeneutics is important for Christian theology in the same way as it is for classical
studies, then neither theological nor classical hermeneutics represents the essence of the matter. Rather, hermeneutics itself is something greater out of which these two
types flow. To be sure, only these two, classical philologians and philological theologians, have contributed to
our discipline. Juristic hermeneutics is a different matter. In the main it is concerned only with determining
the extent of the law, that is, with applying general
principles to particular cases which had not been foreseen
at the time the principles were formulated.

Ast could almost induce me to assert that hermeneutics sould be restricted to these two areas of study. For
at the very beginning of his outline, where he describes
the task of understanding, he leads us up to the very
height of the unity of spirit and concludes that all our
cultural activities are directed toward the unification of
the Greek and Christian life. Thus hermeneutics, too, is
directed to these two alone.[10] And if hermeneutics introduces, on the one hand, the science of antiquity and, on
the other hand, Christian theology, then both studies
would be carried out in the spirit of their unity. Moreover, there would be justification for hermeneutics to
deal both with oriental texts, which represent the common
point of origin for classical and Christian studies, and
with romantic literature, which is clearly close to the

unity of the two. Were oriental and romantic literature regarded as self-contained spheres in the way classical philosophy and Biblical studies are, we would require four hermeneutics, each constructed in a distinctive manner to serve as the organon for its particular discipline. Then, however, there would have to be a still higher organon common to all four.

Now although I want to ascend to this higher sphere, I am afraid of Wolf's shadow. In the few sentences he devotes to hermeneutics Wolf laments that this theory is by no means complete, and he notes that several investigations remain to be undertaken before it can be established. These investigations do not lie on such dizzy heights, but in quite moderate zones. They deal with the meanings of words, the senses of sentences, and the coherence of statements. Yet at the same time he states, as a consolation, that this incompleteness is not too damaging, since the results of these investigations would contribute but little to awaken the talent of the interpreter or to enhance his intellectual ability. Then, as a warning, he refers to the distinction he makes between the type of theories advanced by the ancients, which actually facilitated a task (in this case, the task of interpretation), and those theories to which we moderns are inclined, which become engrossed in abstruse accounts of the nature and bases of the art and so fail to be of any practical value.[11] I fear he was referring to the distinction with which I began. In that case the purely scientific theory is one that will be of no use; the only useful theory is the one that offers an orderly collection of philological observations. Yet, on the one hand, it seems to me that this collection of observations requires something more in order that we may determine the extent to which the rules should be applied. The "modern" kind of theory certainly supplies that. On the other hand, I think that this "modern" kind, even though it deals only with the nature and bases of an art, will always exercise some influence

on the practice of that art. But since I do not want to
endanger the applicability of the theory, I prefer to
leave the speculative guides to their soaring and follow
the practical ones.

These leaders explain above all (although only par-
enthetically and without much emphasis) that hermeneutics
is the art of discovering with necessary insight the
thoughts contained in the work of an author.[12] And this
next assertion salvages much of what I had hoped to gain
by following the more speculative guides: Hermeneutics
does not apply exclusively to classical studies, nor is it
merely a part of this restricted philological organon;
rather, it is to be applied to the works of every author.
Therefore, its principles must be sufficiently general,
and they are not to be derived solely from the nature of
classical literature. Ast makes me uncomfortable with
such a well-formulated statement, but even so I must try
to draw its component parts together.

He begins with the concept of something foreign
which is to be understood. Now, to be sure, he does not
state this concept in its sharpest form. If what is to be
understood were so completely foreign to the one trying to
understand it that there was nothing in common between the
two, then there would be no point of contact for understanding at all.[13] But I conclude that the concept holds
in a relative sense. It then follows that, just as hermeneutics would be unable to begin its work if what is to be
understood were completely foreign, so there would be no
reason for hermeneutics to begin if nothing were strange
between the speaker and hearer. That is, understanding
would always occur immediately upon reading or hearing, or
it would be already given in a divinatory manner, and understanding would take place by itself.

I am quite content to restrict the application of
hermeneutics to the area between these two extremes. But
I must also admit that I want to claim this entire area
for it, meaning that wherever one encounters something

strange in the way thoughts are being expressed in speech,
one is faced with a task which can be solved only with the
help of a theory, presupposing of course some common point
between the speaker and the one who is to understand.

My two guides, however, restrict me at several
points. The one states he is interested only in understanding authors, as though the same problems do not arise
in conversation and direct speech. The other wants to restrict what is "foreign" to something written in a foreign
language, and, more specifically, to works marked by
genius [Werke des Geistes], a sphere even narrower than
that of authors in general.[14] But we can come to learn a
great deal from works which have no outstanding intellectual content, for example, from stories narrated in a
style similar to that normally used in ordinary conversation to tell about minor occurrences, a long way from artistic historical writing, or from letters composed in a
highly intimate and casual style. Even such cases as
these present equally difficult tasks for the work of hermeneutics. Moreover, I submit that Wolf's view is really
not much different than Ast's, and were I to ask him
whether such authors as newspaper reporters or those who
write newspaper advertisements are to be treated by the
science of interpretation, he would not give me a very
friendly response. Although many of these materials are
such that there can be nothing foreign between the author
and the reader, there are exceptions, and I cannot understand why these strange elements can or must be made intelligible in some way other than more artistic writings.
Further, there are other cases (epigrams, for example,
that are not significantly different from newspaper articles) which are impossible to differentiate into two classes, or two different methods or theories. Indeed, I must
reiterate that hermeneutics is not to be limited to written texts. I often make use of hermeneutics in personal
conversation when, discontented with the ordinary level of
understanding, I wish to explore how my friend has moved

from one thought to another or try to trace out the views, judgments, and aspirations which led him to speak about a given subject in just this way and no other. No doubt everyone has such experiences, and I think they make it clear that the task for which we seek a theory is not limited to what is fixed in writing but arises whenever we have to understand a thought or series of thoughts expressed in words.

Nor is the hermeneutical task restricted to a foreign language. Even in our native language, and without considering the various dialects of the language or the peculiarities of a person's speech, the thoughts and expressions of another person, whether written or spoken, contain strange elements. Indeed, I readily acknowledge that I consider the practice of hermeneutics occurring in immediate communication in one's native language very essential for our cultured life, apart from all philological or theological studies. Who could move in the company of exceptionally gifted persons without endeavoring to hear "between" their words, just as we read between the lines of original and tightly written books? Who does not try in a meaningful conversation, which may in certain respects be an important act, to lift out its main points, to try to grasp its internal coherence, to pursue all its subtle intimations further? Wolf--especially Wolf, who was such an artist in conversation, but who said more by intimation than by explicit statement, and even more by innuendo--would not deny that these were being understood by his listeners in an artistic way, so that he could count on the audience always knowing what he meant. Should the way we observe and interpret experienced, worldly-wise and politically shrewd persons really differ from the procedure we use with books? Should it be so different that it would depend on entirely different principles and be incapable of a comparably developed and orderly presentation? That I do not believe. On the contrary, I see two different applications of the same art.

In the one application certain motives are more prominent, while others remain in the background; and in the other the relationship is just the reverse. In fact, I would go even further and assert that the two applications are so closely related that neither can be practiced without the other. To be specific, however, and to deal with matters which are most similar to the interpretation of written works, I would strongly recommend diligence in interpreting significant conversations. The immediate presence of the speaker, the living expression that proclaims that his whole being is involved, the way the thoughts in a conversation develop from our shared life, such factors stimulate us far more than some solitary observation of an isolated text to understand a series of thoughts as a moment of life which is breaking forth, as one moment set in the context of many others. And this dimension of understanding is often slighted, in fact, almost completely neglected, in interpreting authors. When we compare the two, it would be better say that we see two parts rather than two forms of the task. To be sure, when something strange in a language blocks our understanding, we must try to overcome the difficulty. But even if we do come to understand this strange element, we may still find ourselves blocked because we cannot grasp the coherence of what someone is saying. And if neither approach is able to overcome the difficulty, the problem may well go unsolved.

To return then to the explanations we mentioned above, I must first lodge a protest against Wolf's claim that hermeneutics should ascertain the thoughts of an author with a necessary insight.[15] I do not mean to suggest that I consider this demand too stringent. To the contrary, for many cases it is not too stringent at all. Yet I am afraid that by stating the task in these terms, many cases for which this formulation of the problem is simply not appropriate would be passed over, and I do not want them to be overlooked. There are, of course, many instances in which one can prove that a given word in its

context must mean "this" and nothing else, although such
proof is difficult to find without recourse to those investigations into the nature of word-meanings which Wolf,
perhaps too summarily, has rejected. And, taking up a position somewhere outside of this circle, one may put together a number of these elementary proofs in order to arrive at a satisfactory proof of the sense of a sentence.
But how many other cases there are--and they are crucial
for interpreting the New Testament, especially--where a
necessary insight is impossible, and interpreters come to
equally probable meanings according to their points of
view. Even in the field of criticism it often happens
that some know no other way to oppose the result of a
thorough investigation than to claim that some other meaning is still "possible." Of course, in the long run such
remonstrances do not accomplish very much, but until each
and every such possibility has been definitively eliminated, there can be no talk of a necessary insight. And if
we go further and remember how advisable it is to undertake the difficult task of establishing the coherence of
thoughts in the larger sections of the text, and to ascertain the hidden supplements of, as it were, lost intimations, then understanding is not only, as Wolf portrays
it, a matter of collating and summarizing minute historical moments. Rather it becomes sensitive to the particular way an author combines the thoughts, for had those
thoughts been formulated differently, even in the same
historical situation and the same kind of presentation,
the result would have been different. In such cases we
may be fully convinced of our view, and it may even be
convincing to our contemporaries who are engaged in similar studies. Nonetheless, it would be futile to try to
pass this account off as a demonstration. This is not
said to disparage such studies, but in this area, especially, we may cite the otherwise rather paradoxical words
of a distinguished scholar who has only recently been tak-
en from us: an assertion is much more than a proof.[16]

Moreover, there exists a completely different sort of certainty than the critical one for which Wolf is praised, namely, a divinatory certainty which arises when an interpreter delves as deeply as possible into an author's state of mind [Verfassung].[17] Thus it is often the case, as the Platonic rhapsodist admits, though quite naively, that he is able to offer an outstanding interpretation of Homer, but frequently cannot shed light on other writers, whether poets or prosaists.[18] For, provided the knowledge is available to him, an interpreter can and should show himself to be equally competent in every area related to language and to the historical situation of a people and of an age. Yet, just as in life we are most successful in understanding our friends, so a skillful interpreter is most successful in correctly interpreting an author's process of drafting and composing a work, the product of his personal distinctiveness in language and in all his relationships, when the author is among those favorites with whom he is best acquainted. For works of other authors, however, an interpreter will content himself with knowing less about these things; he will not feel ashamed to seek help from colleagues who are closer to them. In fact, it might be maintained that the entire practice of interpretation is to be divided as follows. One class of interpreters deals more with the language and with history than with personalities, granting equal consideration to all of the authors who write in a given language, regardless of the fact that the authors excel in different areas. A second class of interpreters, however, deals primarily with the observation of persons, regarding the language merely as the medium by which persons express their history and as the modality within which they exist. Thus each interpreter limits himself to that writer who is most readily understandable to him. This description may well be accurate except that writers of the latter group come less frequently to public attention because their work is less susceptible to polemical discussions, and they enjoy

the fruits of each other's labors in quiet contentment.
Still, several passages indicate that Wolf has by no means
completely overlooked this side of interpretation, but, at
least in part, has taken into account that certainty which
we have described as more divinatory than demonstrable.
It is worthwhile for us to investigate one of these places
more closely.

In his Compendium Ast presents grammar, hermeneutics
and criticism together as correlated disciplines without
adding anything else as related knowledge. But we have no
way of comprehending how they are interrelated because he
relegates them to an appendix.[19] Wolf, however, does not
consider these three alone sufficient for an organon of
the science of antiquity, but adds to them fluency in
style and the art of composition, which, because it includes poetry, involves classical meter.[20] At first
glance this is very surprising. For my own part I would
have been content to have understood the fluency in ancient styles of writing--and in the case of the languages
of antiquity this is the only aspect of composition we are
discussing--as the mature fruit of long-term studies in
the science of antiquity. For one must have lived just as
fully and vigorously in the ancient world as in the present, and one must be keenly aware of all the forms of human existence and of the special nature of the surrounding
objects at that time, in order to excel in weaving such
graceful patterns based on set formulae and to form in
Roman and Hellenistic ideas works which can affect us
deeply even today, and to reproduce these in the most ancient way possible. How then can Wolf demand such art
from us as the admission fee, so to speak, to the shrine
of the science of antiquity? And by what honest means are
we supposed to obtain it? Assuming there is no magical
way, I see no other than that of tradition and that of
adopting a procedure that is, fortunately, not merely imi-
tative, but also divinatory--methods that would ultimately
lead to fluency as the fruit of study. This path leads us

in a kind of circle, for we cannot gain a style of writing
Latin--for which we must know Greek as well--in the same
immediate way as those who, by virtue of having Latin and
Greek as their native languages, developed their stylistic
fluency from their immediate existence and not from such
studies as these. Nor had I expected Wolf to demand a
knowledge of meter. It seemed to me that this was one of
the more specialized aspects of the science of antiquity
rather than an essential part of the ancient theory of
art. It had as much to do with the science of orchestra-
tion as with the science of poetry, and the theory of
prose rhythm and declamation which was drawn from it represents the whole development of the national temper as
shown in the character of artistic movements.

But let us put meter aside, for regardless of what
is involved in one's fluency in ancient composition, the
true key to this Wolfian research is the following: Wolf
does not require this fluency directly for the specialized
disciplines of the science of antiquity, but for hermeneutics, that is, for gaining a correct and complete understanding in the higher sense of the term. And although he
does not especially emphasize it, it is obvious, with respect to both criticism and meter, that his entry to the
shrine of the science of antiquity is founded on two
steps. The lower step is grammer, in his view the foundation of hermeneutics and criticism, and the fluency of
style. The higher step is hermeneutics and criticism.
Now just as Wolf sets forth his grammar in great detail
and not in the elementary way which we could use with beginning students, so, too, we may be certain that by the
fluency of style he is not referring to the Latin exercises done in our high schools, which are skilled imitations and applications of grammatical knowledge. But
since it is also certain that only a person who has worked
through the entire literature of antiquity could perform
the actual operations which the ancients did in the two
languages in a free and individual fashion, is it perhaps

possible that this great scholar is referring to something other than a knowledge of the various forms of presentation, their limits and possibilities, which is acquired by actual practice?[21] And this other element is of great influence on that less demonstrable aspect of the art of interpretation which is oriented toward the internal intellectual activity of an author. Herewith a new understanding of this side of interpretation is opened to us, and surely Wolf had it in mind, even though he did not give it much emphasis at the beginning of his exposition.[22]

In essence, then, the matter is as follows. When we view, on the one hand, the different forms of outstanding oratorical art and, on the other hand, the different types of style used for scientific and commercial activities which have developed in a language, it is evident that the entire history of literature is divided into two contrasting periods, the characteristics of which may later reappear simultaneously, but only in a subordinate fashion. The first period is that in which these forms are gradually developed; the second is that in which they predominate. And if the task of hermeneutics is to reproduce the whole internal process of an author's way of combining thoughts, then it is necessary to know with as much certainty as possible to which of these two periods he belongs. For if an author belongs to the first period, he was creating purely from his own resources, and from the intensity of his production and his linguistic power we may conclude not only that he produced a distinctive work, but that to a certain extent he originated a new type of work, which persists in the language. The same thing may be said, although not in such strong terms, about every author who especially modified these forms, introduced new elements in them, or founded a new style in them. However, the more a writer belongs in the second period and so does not produce the form but composes works in forms which are already established, the more we must know these forms in order to understand his activity. Even in the

initial conception of a work, an author is guided by the
established form. Its power affects the arrangement and
organization of the works, and its particular laws close
off certain areas of language and certain modifications of
ideas, and opens up others. Thus the power of the form
modifies not only the expression, but also--and the two
can never be fully separated--the content. Consequently,
an interpreter who does not see correctly how the stream
of thinking and composing at once crash against and recoil
from the walls of its bed and is diverted into a course
other than it would have taken by itself cannot correctly
understand the internal movement of the composition. Even
less can he ascertain the author's true relation to the
language and to its forms. He will not become aware of
how an author may have more fully and forcefully expressed
the images and thought which inspired him had he not been
restricted by a form which in many respects conflicted
with his personal individuality. He will not know how to
assess correctly an author who would not have ventured
very far into a genre had he not stood within the protec-
tive and guiding power of a form, for a form may aid as
well as limit an author. And of the two kinds of authors
he will not sufficiently appreciate the one who, rather
than struggle with a form, is stimulated just as freely by
an existing form as if he had just produced it himself.
This insight into an author's relationship to the forms
imbedded in his literature is such an essential aspect of
interpretation that without it neither the whole nor the
parts can be correctly understood. There is no doubt, of
course, that Wolf is right to maintain that an interpreter
cannot "divine" correctly unless he himself has experienced how an author can work within the given limits and
rules which exist in a language and how he may struggle
against them.[23] And though here as elsewhere the comparative operation is set over against the divinatory, it cannot replace it completely. For how are we to find a point
for beginning the comparative operation if it is not given

by a proper search? And it is for this reason that meter
is to be considered, since the emphasis on the syllables
of a poetical composition is essentially a matter of
choosing expressions and since the position of the
thoughts is conditioned by the form. And it is in the influence which this exercises on the work that the different relations to the clearest passages are to be found.
Yet in all the languages with which we are dealing here
the relationship between the content and the form during
the process of composition is essentially and in the main
the same. And so I would not insist as strongly as Wolf
that the training necessary for interpretation must be acquired solely from practice in the ancient languages.[24]
Were that necessary, I would not be able to understand why
the Roman language was able to supplant the Greek.

I want to underscore here a consideration about the
character which these exercises will always display when
we apply ourselves to the thoughts in the literature of a
given language, because several significant conclusions
are to be developed from what has been written above. We
must remember that whenever we practice this art, we must
remain conscious of both methods, the divinatory and the
comparative. This rule is so universal that, on the one
hand, we can regard an immediate understanding, in which
no particular mediating activities can be detected, as a
temporarily indistinguishable combination and interaction
of the two methods and, on the other hand, we can see that
even the most complex applications of the art of interpretation involve nothing other than a constant shifting from
the one method to the other. In this interaction the results of the one method must approximate more and more
those of the other. Otherwise, very few satisfactory conclusions can be gained. This distinction between the more
grammatical aspect, which aims at understanding the discourse in terms of the totality of language, and the more
psychological aspect, which aims at understanding the discourse in terms of a continuous production of thoughts, is

based on the following premise. Just as both methods are
necessary to obtain complete understanding, so every combination of the two must proceed in such a way that the
initial result of the one method will be supplemented by
further applications of the other.

We must ask, then, whether these two methods apply
to both the grammatical and technical aspects of interpretation, or whether each method is appropriate for only one
aspect? For example, when Wolf, on the basis of the role
he assigns to meter and fluency in composition, tries to
argue that only a comparative procedure can be used for
the more psychological aspect of interpretation, is he implying that the other, more grammatical aspect, must be
furthered by the divinatory method? His essay does not
provide us with a direct and definitive answer to this
question. But his investigations into the meanings of
words and the senses of sentences, although not organized
in a very helpful fashion, evidently have to do only with
the grammatical aspect of interpretation and require a
comparative method.[25]

An examination of the task itself leads to the same
conclusion. All grammatical difficulties are overcome by
a comparative operation alone, by repeatedly comparing
what is already understood with what is not yet understood, so that what is not understood is confined within
even narrower bounds. And, on the other side, the finest
fruit of all esthetic criticism of artistic works is a
heightened understanding of the intimate operations of
poets and other artists of language by means of grasping
their entire process of composition, from its conception
up to the final execution. Indeed, if there is any truth
to the dictum that the height of understanding is to understand an author better than he understood himself, this
must be it. And in our literature we possess a considerable number of critical works which have performed this
task with good success.[26] But how is such success possible except by a comparative procedure which helps us gain

a thorough understanding about where and how an author has
gone beyond or lagged behind others, and in what respects
his kind of work is related to or different from theirs?
Nonetheless, it is certain that the grammatical side of
interpretation cannot dispense with the divinatory method.
For whenever we come upon a gifted author [genialer Autor]
who has for the first time in the history of the language
expressed a given phrase or combination of terms, what do
we want to do? In such instances only a divinatory method
enables us rightly to reconstruct the creative act that
begins with the generation of thoughts which captivate the
author and to understand how the requirement of the moment
could draw upon the living treasure of words in the author's mind in order to produce just this way of putting
it and no other. But here, too, our conclusions will be
uncertain unless the comparative operation is applied to
the psychological aspect.

Therefore, we must answer the question before us as
follows. If our first reading of a text does not immediately give us a certain and complete understanding, then
we must employ both methods in both aspects--though naturally in varying degrees according to the difference of
their objects--until the result approximates as nearly as
possible that of immediate understanding. We surely must
accept what I have said about one class of interpreters
inclining more to the psychological and another to the
grammatical aspect. We know that many a virtuoso in grammatical interpretation gives scant attention to the internal process of combining thoughts in one's mind and feeling. And, vice versa, there are fine interpreters who reflect about the special relationship of a text to its language only minimally and then only in those rare cases
when they are forced to consult a dictionary. If we take
this into account and apply it equally to the two methods,
we must conclude that just as we can regard immediate and
instantaneous understanding as having arisen in either
way, thus directing our attention to the author's crea-

tivity or to the objective totality of the language, so we
can regard the successful completion of a more artful
method in interpretation in these same terms. We can now
say that all of the points of comparison, for the psychological as well as for the grammatical aspects, have been
brought together so perfectly that we no longer need to
consider the divinatory method and its results. We can
then add that the divinatory operation has been conducted
with such thoroughness and precision that the comparative
method is rendered superfluous. Likewise, the internal
process has been made so transparent by the divinatory and
the comparative methods that, since what has been intuited
is a thought, and there is no thought without words, the
entire relationship between the production of the thoughts
and its formation in language is now fully and immediately
evident. But the reverse would also be true.

Yet, even as I am dealing here with the completion
of the operation, I am driven back almost involuntarily to
the very beginning in order to encompass the whole within
these two points. This very beginning, however, is the
same as when children begin to understand language. How,
then, do our formulae apply to these beginnings? Children
do not yet have language, but are seeking it. Nor do they
know the activity of thinking, because there is no thinking without words. With what aspect, then, do they begin?
They do not yet have any points of comparison, but they
acquire them gradually as a foundation for a comparative
operation that, to be sure, develops remarkably fast. Are
we not tempted to say that each child produces both thinking and language originally, and that either each child
out of himself by virtue of an inner necessity engenders
them in a way that coincides with the way it had happened
in others or gradually as he becomes capable of a comparative procedure he approximates others. But in fact this
inner movement toward producing thoughts on one's own, although initially stimulated by others, is the same as that
which we have called "the divinatory." This divinatory

operation, therefore, is original, and the soul [die
Seele] shows itself to be wholly and inherently a presci-
ent being [ein ahndendes Wesen]. But with what an enor-
mous, almost infinite, power of expression does the child
begin! It cannot be likened to later developments, nor to
anything else. The two ways must be grasped simultaneously as essentially one, since each supports the other, and
only gradually are the two distinguished, as the language
objectifies itself by fixing particular words to objects
and to images which themselves become increasingly clear
and certain. But at the same time the act of thinking is
able--how should I say it--to use these in order to reproduce them, or to reproduce them in order to grasp them.
These first activities of thinking and knowing are so astonishing that it seems to me that when we smile at the
false applications which children make of the elements of
language they have acquired--and to be sure often with all
too great consistency--we do so only in order to find consolation or even to take revenge for this excess of energy
which we are no longer able to expend.

Viewed in this light, whenever we do not understand
we find ourselves in the same situation as the children,
although not to the same degree. Even in what is familiar
we encounter something that is unusual in the language,
when a combination of words does not become evident to us,
when a train of thought strikes us as odd, even though it
is analogous to our own, [or] when the connection between
the various parts of a train of thought or its extension
remains uncertain and hovers unsteadily before us. On
such occasions, we can always begin with the same divinatory boldness. Therefore, we ought not simply contrast
our present situation to those immense beginnings in
childhood, for the process of understanding and interpret-
ting is a whole which develops constantly and gradually,
and in its later stages we must aid each other more and
more, since each of us offers to others points of comparison and similarities which themselves begin in this same

divinatory way. This is the gradual self-discovery of the thinking self. But, just as the circulation of blood and the rhythm of breathing gradually diminish, so the soul, too, the more it possesses, becomes more sluggish, in inverse proportion to its receptivity. This is true of even the most active people. Since each person, as an individual, is the not-being of the other, it is never possible to eliminate non-understanding completely. But although the speed of the hermeneutical operation diminishes after its early stages, a more deliberate movement and a longer duration of each aspect enhance the process.

Finally there comes that period when hermeneutical experiences are collected and become guidelines--for I prefer to call them this rather than rules. A technical theory, however, cannot develop, as should be obvious from what I have said, until we have penetrated the language of an author in its objectivity and the process of producing thoughts, as a function of the life of the individual mind, in relationship to the nature of thinking. For only in these terms can the way thoughts are combined and communicated and the way understanding takes place be explicated in a fully coherent fashion.

Yet in order to clarify fully the relationship between these two operations, we must give due attention first to a notion which seems to give Ast the advantage over Wolf, although until we fully determine the form of hermeneutics from it, it seems to be more a discovery than an invention. This is the notion that any part of a text can be understood only by means of an understanding of the whole, and that for this reason every explanation of a given element already presupposes that the whole has been understood.[27]

The Second Address

Read on October 29.

The hermeneutical principle which Ast has proposed and in several respects developed quite extensively is

that just as the whole is understood from the parts, so
the parts can be understood only from the whole. This
principle is of such consequence for hermeneutics and so
incontestable that one cannot even begin to interpret
without using it.

Indeed, a great number of hermeneutical rules are to
a greater or lesser extent based on it. Each word has a
certain range of meanings, but what part of this range occurs in a given passage and what parts are excluded are
determined by the other parts of speech in the sentence
and especially by those parts of speech most closely or
organically related to it. This means that the word is
understood both as a part of a whole range of meanings and
as a special meaning with a given context. This is the
case for words that have a variety of so-called meanings,
words that are capable of different levels of meaning, and
words that are emphasized to varying degrees.

Accordingly, the rule that a word which occurs twice
in the same context should be explained the same way in
both instances is sound, for it is improbable that an author would have used the word differently in the two instances.[28] This rule, however, holds only under the condition that the sentence in which the word occurs the second time can legitimately be considered a part of the same
context. In certain circumstances an author will use a
word differently in a new context, just as he would in another work. So, if the meaning a word has the first time
determines the meaning it has in its second appearance,
the part is understood from the whole, for the explanation
depends on our certainty that this section of the text is,
with reference to the word in question, a whole. Likewise, the proper way to treat parallel instances of a word
is to select only those passages that provide a similar
context for explaining the word in question. That is,
they represent parts of the same whole. Insofar as this
is not certain the resulting explanation will be questionable.

Although this account is quite intelligible--and it could be confirmed by additional examples--it is still difficult to decide how far one should go in applying this rule. Just as the word in a sentence is a particular and a part, so, too, is the sentence in the larger context of a text. Consequently, we very easily get completely mistaken ideas [Vorstellungen] from sentences that have been extracted from their context and inserted into another as snippets or as sayings. The use of such citations is so common that it is only astonishing that trust in them has not become universal. Of course, it is another matter entirely with statements that may be appropriately used as aphorisms. Even so, taken in isolation, these, too, always seem quite vague, and their precise meaning comes from the context into which they are introduced. Actually, much of their special charm is due to their ability to enrich such a variety of contexts, and though they more easily stand alone because of their aphoristic form, the context modifies their meaning each time they are used.

To proceed a step further, this rule may be applied to combinations of sentences. No doubt this is the reason, for example, that we Germans are so often accused of not understanding persiflage, which always extends through a series of sentences. Such a misunderstanding is the author's fault when he fails to provide any indicators and the serious reading seems altogether adequate; but it is the reader's fault when he overlooks the clues present in the text and fails to discern how this set of sentences is related to the whole.

Yet the problem is by no means limited to such instances as persiflage. Wherever the understanding of a series of sentences and their interconnection is in question, one must first and foremost know the whole to which they belong. Indeed, since this case, too, can be traced back to the original principle, the principle must hold universally. In fact, every highly coherent set of sentences is governed by a dominant concept, though the way

this concept "governs" the text will vary according to the
type of work. This concept, just as a word in a given
sentence, can be fully determined only when it is read in
its context. That is, any set of sentences, large or
small, can be understood correctly only in terms of the
whole to which it belongs. And just as the shorter sets
of sentences are conditioned by larger sets, so, too,
these larger sets are conditioned by still larger ones.
Thus the obvious conclusion is that any part can be completely understood only through the whole.

When we consider the task of interpretation with
this principle in mind, we have to say that our increasing
understanding of each sentence and of each section, an understanding which we achieve by starting at the beginning
and moving forward slowly, is always provisional. It becomes more complete as we are able to see each larger section as a coherent unity. But as soon as we turn to a new
part we encounter new uncertainties and begin again, as it
were, in the dim morning light. It is like starting all
over, except that as we push ahead the new material illu-
mines everything we have already treated, until suddenly
at the end every part is clear and the whole work is visi-
ble in sharp and definite contours.[29]

We cannot quarrel with Ast when he tries to overcome
this constant backtracking and beginning anew by advising
us to begin with a presentiment of the whole. But how are
we to gain such a presentiment?[30] Of course, if we limit
our task to written works, as both Wolf and Ast apparently
intended, it is possible to gain such a presentiment.
Prefaces, which are seldom given in oral presentations,
are more helpful than mere titles. Moreover, we demand
that certain types of books present summaries of the sections and tables of contents, not only to allow readers to
locate particular points easily but even more to provide
them with an overview that enables them to see how the
work is structured and to identify these key words which
govern the various parts. The more help of this kind we

have, the easier it is to follow Ast's advice. And even
when such aids are entirely missing, if only the text is
before us, we can resort to that practice, so distasteful
to look at, of thumbing through the pages of a book before
reading it in earnest. If one is lucky or has a knack for
this sort of thing, it may be of considerable use in com-
pensating for the lack of help from the author. Nonetheless, when I think of the people of antiquity, I am almost
ashamed to say such a thing. They were condemned to use
the same rules of understanding as we, but they knew nothing of such aids or tricks. Indeed, some of the most outstanding prose works were so composed that such aids were
not only omitted but would have been disdained and that
the unavoidable external divisions of the work were not
related at all to the actual organization from which a
presentiment of the whole could be gained. In poetic
works anything hinting of such aids is almost laughable.
Finally, there are still a few among us who are sufficiently noble to let others read to them, and they do not
thumb through the pages, nor are they helped by tables of
contents. How, then, are we supposed to arrive at this
presentiment of the whole without which an understanding
of the parts is impossible? We must try to answer this
question in the most general way.

It must first be said that not every text is a whole
in the same sense. Some texts are only loose series of
statements. In these cases understanding a particular
part in terms of the whole is not possible at all. Other
texts are only a loose succession of smaller units. In
these cases particular points must be understood from the
units of which they are a part. Which of these is the
case with a given discourse or text depends on the genre
to which it belongs, and of course even within a given
genre there are numerous gradations. One author will develop his work in strict adherence to the specifications
of a genre, whereas another will be extremely flexible in
his use of those specifications. Our first inkling of how

an author deals with a genre is gained from our general
acquaintance with the author and his way of writing. In
the case of speeches which are not available to us in
written form and so can be heard only once, our provisional grasp of the whole cannot extend beyond what we can
gather from our general knowledge of the genre and from
our acquaintance with the speaker and his habits, unless
the speaker himself gives us an overview of what he is
going to say. If we are not familiar with a given genre
and with the speaker, we must draw our conclusions about
the whole from the way the speaker accents and constructs
the material and the way he develops it as he proceeds.
Even when a provisional grasp of the whole is not possible, we may still come to understand the whole from the
parts. Such an understanding, however, will necessarily
be incomplete unless we remember the parts clearly and are
able, once the entire speech has been delivered, to refer
back to them in order to understand them more precisely
and more fully from the whole. Consequently, the difference between oral and written statements disappears, because in dealing with the former our memory supplies all
of the information that the written form alone seemed to
insure. Thus, as Plato said long ago, we need to write
only to make up for defects in our memory, a vicious
circle, since writing arises from the corruption of the
memory and further corrupts the memory.[31]

It follows from what I have said that for both
speeches and written texts our initial grasp of the whole
is only provisional and imperfect. It is, as it were, a
more orderly and complete way to thumb pages, but it is
adequate and equal to the task only so long as we do not
encounter anything strange and understanding takes place
by itself, that is, where no hermeneutical operation is
performed consciously. In all other cases, however, we
must shift from the ending back to the beginning and im-
prove our initial grasp of the work by starting all over
again. The more difficult it is to grasp how the entire

text has been organized, the more we will develop our conception by working on the parts. The richer and more significant the parts are, the more we will develop our conception by means of a view of the whole in all its relations. To be sure, almost every work contains certain parts that cannot be fully understood in relation to the overall organization of the text because they, as it were, lie outside of the textual organization and so can be called secondary thoughts. They could just as easily occur in another text as in this one, and were they developed as major thoughts they might require an entirely different type of work. But to some degree at least these secondary thoughts, as freely expressed convictions of the author, though determined by a momentary occasion, do constitute a whole, not so much in relation to the genre of the work as to the individuality of the author. Therefore, they contribute less to our understanding of the text as a living and organized expression of the language than as a creative moment of the author.

Just as those texts in which the whole is evident from the parts or in which, given even the faintest outlines of the whole, the parts can be surmised offer the most simple task for determining the relationship between the whole and the parts, so the most difficult ones are those great works of the creative spirit, whatever their form and genre, each of which in its own way is organized in infinite detail and at the same time is inexhaustible in each of its parts. Every solution to the task of understanding appears to us as only an approximation. Our understanding would be complete only if we could proceed with such works as we do with those we have designated as minimal in this respect, that is, if we could solve the problems of the organization of the whole and the parts at least in a relatively similar way. If we reflect on this, we certainly find a powerful reason why Wolf demands a skill in composition as an almost indispensable condition for the interpreter as well as for the critic.[32] For it may be well nigh impossible in this task to substitute a

large selection of analogies for the divinatory method,
which is awakened mainly by one's own productivity.

Yet, not content with the range of the task as previously described, Ast shows us a way to raise it to a
still higher power, and this way is not to be disdained.
Just as a word relates to a sentence, a sentence to a section, and a section to a work as a particular to a totality or a part to a whole, so, too, every speech and every
text is a particular or part that can be completely understood only in relation to a still larger whole.[33] It is
easy to see that every work represents just such a particular or part in two respects. First, each work is a part
of the sphere of literature to which it belongs, and together with other works of similar merit it forms a body
of literature. This body of literature helps one to interpret each work with reference to the language. Second,
each work is also a part of the author's life, and together with his other acts it forms the totality of his life.
Thus it is to be understood only from the totality of the
person's acts, inasmuch as it is of influence upon his
life and is in keeping with it. There will always be a
considerable difference--though greater or lesser depend-
ing on how the work was created--between a reader who acquires an understanding of the work in the way I have described and a reader who has accompanied the author
throughout his entire life up to the appearance of the
work. This latter reader, far more than the former, has
a clearer and more definite view of how the author's personality steps forward in the course of the work as well
as in each of its parts. A similar distinction may be
made between that reader and one who is acquainted with
the entire circle of related literature and can therefore
assess in an entirely different way the linguistic values
of the various parts and the technical aspects of the entire linguistic complex. Thus whatever is said about the
smallest parts of a work may be applied to the entire
work, for it, too, is part of an even larger whole.

Even after we have revised our initial concept of a work, our understanding is still only provisional, and a text is placed in an entirely different light when, after reading through all of the literature related to it and after acquainting ourselves with other, even quite different, works by the same author and, as much as possible, with his entire life, we return to the work in question. Thus, if we are to understand the various parts of a work in terms of the whole, tables of contents and schematic overviews cannot take the place of reworking our initial conceptions or turning back from the ending to the beginning. This procedure is indispensable, both because it enables us to free ourselves from reliance on the opinions of others, which can mislead us before we are able to detect their flaws, and because none of these aids is perspicuous enough to arouse in a lively way the divinatory talent, which is most important.

Likewise, when it is a question of understanding a work from both the related literature and the total activity of the author, substituting prolegomena and commentaries for these procedures will be of little avail. Usually, a study of related works only helps us to see what the author has used, and vice versa, and only a knowledge of the author himself, his acts and his relationships, enables us to see what importance they may have had on the work. Thus such study helps us only to deal with the part and not at all with the whole. A vivid and reliable characterization of the author which draws on his entire life or a morphology of the genre which compares entire groups of texts in order to gain a comprehensive understanding of those groups which perhaps were first brought in relation to a given author or genre by this work itself would not be appropriate to deal with the specific character and intent of this work.

Although these statements seem to express the highpoint of the demand that we understand the parts from the whole, we would not want to forget what was said still earlier. Although it was mentioned only in passing, you will recall the statement that there are two classes of interpreters who can be distinguished by their procedures. The one class directs its attention almost exclusively to the linguistic relations of a given text. The other pays more attention to the original psychic process of producing and combining ideas and images.

At this point we can see with special clarity the difference in talents. Linguistically-oriented interpreters try to comprehend a work by grasping how it is related to similar works of the same type. They focus on the forms of composition which arise from the nature of the language and of the common life which develops and is bound together with language. Thus the individual and personal elements which emerge here are those which have become most universal, and so these elements receive least attention. The other interpreters, however, want to determine from a composition what kind of person the author is. To do this they identify themselves as much as possible with the moments of creativity and conception which break into the fabric of the author's everyday life like higher inspirations. They seek a vivid insight into every facet of the parts that may illuminate the process of creation, including secondary thoughts which were of no consequence for the idea of the work, in order to evaluate properly how the whole process of composition is related to the author's existence or how the author's personality develops itself in representations. Of course, for such interpreters the relation to the language mentioned above recedes into the background.

Full understanding requires both of these operations, and no interpreter can fully understand if he leans so much to one side that he is completely unable to make use of what the other side offers. An interpreter in the latter class who wanted only to dabble in linguistic matters would make many mistakes, no matter how much he might love to understand the author and no matter how much he

might guard against imputing intentions to the author
which the author did not have in mind, as such interpreters tend to do. The more significant the author was for
the development of the language, the more errors would be
committed. In our own field of interest we have to call
such an interpreter by a name that has been used, not
without appropriateness, in the sphere of artistic produc-
tivity--I take this generally to include the poet and
speaker and even the philosopher as well as the artist: he
is a "nebulist." Or consider an interpreter of the other
type, even one who ascertains how a work is related to
others of its genre with such precision that, not satisfied with discerning sharp comparisons and juxtapositions,
he also has a profound grasp of their significance. Because such an interpreter does not see the whole man in
the work and does not participate in his life, indeed is
incapable of doing so, he cannot avoid what we call "pedantry." Since it is easier to use the works of others to
compensate for one's own deficiencies than to acquire for
oneself techniques for which one has no aptitude, it seems
that those who scale the mountain that rises before us
from the one side are less valuable as interpreters in
their own right than as resources for others. And we
might advise all those who want to be interpreters to work
at both sides, even at the expense of virtuosity at
either, in order to avoid one-sidedness.

Since we have distinguished these two sides of our
enterprise from the outset and have found, in connection
with them, two methods, the divinatory and the comparative, we need now to inquire how the two are related to
the higher level of understanding. Earlier, when we were
limiting our discussion to a given work, we saw that both
operations were necessary for each side, for the grammatical as well as for the psychological. But now, on account
of particular problems with the language, we have to deal
not only with passages from other texts, but with a whole
sphere of literary production. At the same time, our

concern is no longer merely to discover what developed
from the author's original, creative conception of a work,
but thoroughly to consider how it actually developed from
the unity and total context of this particular life.

Thus it may seem that these two methods are no longer given equal weight. If, once again, we pursue both
sides of our task to their conclusions, the one side seems
so underdeveloped and thin in comparison with the other
that it would seem completely improper to give it a place
equal to the other in a new hermeneutics. To confine ourselves to classical antiquity, which remains the primary
field for the art of hermeneutics, we see that we know so
little about the life and existence of so many of the most
important authors that we always wonder how much we can
trust them. Outside of their works themselves, does our
knowledge of Sophocles and Euripides supply us even the
most limited explanation for the differences in their compositions? Or take such well-known men as Plato and Aris-
totle. Does what we know of their lives and relationships
explain even in the most minimal way why the former took
one course in philosophy and the latter another, or to
what extent they may have reconciled their differences in
writings no longer available to us? Indeed, is there any
other ancient whom we know as well as Cicero? He is, I
believe, the only man of antiquity for whom we have a
treasury of personal letters, as actual documents of his
personality, entirely distinct from his major works. If
we turn now to the production of the distant and hazy
Orient, how is it possible to think of trying to distinguish the forms of particular human beings in order to il-
lumine their works by reference to the special way in
which their inner life [Gemüth] developed? The harvest of
such material is sparse even for those earlier witnesses
in our own land that we have only recently begun to study
scientifically. It is only as we approach our own era and
restrict ourselves to the European scene we know so well
and where we all stroll, as it were, in the same hall that

it seems possible to undertake this mode of treatment with sufficient resources for a reasonable degree of success.

Moreover, how trivial this method looks in comparison to the other one! The latter method always leads us to further material, and just when we think we have mastered all the literature related to a given work we find another piece, a part of the same great whole, that promises an even better measuring rod and an even more certain result. The former method, however, always restricts us to the narrow confines of an individual's life, and the most we can expect from our taxing, multifarious effort is a clear picture of this person's life. Nonetheless, even the finest historical reconstruction which we undertake in order to comprehend better a work of some author will achieve true excellence not merely because it clarifies the work in question but also because it enriches our own lives and the lives of others. Such enrichment is sublime, and it should be added to our consideration of works so that we do not produce trivialities which demean ourselves and our scientific labor. Thus a knowledge of a given person as such is not the aim of this side of our task, but a means of enabling us to master the author's activities and so of leading us to an objective consideration of his way of thinking. There can be no doubt that people in classical antiquity were no less concerned with the author as a person, and we must presume that the original readers could come to an understanding that we can only envy because we no longer possess the resources for it. This much, however, is certain from these remarks: in the psychological task we cannot avoid giving greater emphasis to divination, for it is entirely natural for people to construct for themselves a complete image of a person from only scattered traces. But we cannot be too careful in examining from every angle a picture that has been sketched in such a hypothetical fashion. We should accept it only when we find no contradictions, and even then only provisionally. But no one who neglects this side of the hermeneutical task can do justice to a work, for whether a work is integral to an author's intellectual life or is occasioned merely by special circumstances, whether it is a prelude to some greater work or a polemic, is of greatest import to the interpreter.

The other method is by its very nature predominately comparative. Only by taking a number of works together and observing their similarities and differences can one form a general picture of the genre and ascertain how the work in question is related to the genre. But even so there is originally a measure of divination in the way one poses the question about a work, and until the interpreter has determined fully the work's place in the overall group to which it belongs he should not fail to leave a certain field of play for the divinatory method.

If it is a mistake, though I do not think it is, to assign both of these tasks to the interpreter, then it is my fault alone, for my guides do not accept this view any more than they accept what I said earlier. Indeed, I must acknowledge that I have conceived the comparative side of the task differently than Ast. Although he wants to understand a work as a whole from a larger context, the body of literature in which the work is included is for him both too unwieldy and too restrictive to serve as that context. Since he confines himself to classical literature, he advances the formula that a work should be understood out of the spirit of antiquity. This formula could be viewed as an abbreviation of the method which I have presented. For this spirit would be that which commonly dwells in all productions of the same time, and it is identified by abstracting from the works of a given type whatever is distinctive to each individual work. But Ast specifically objects to this procedure. He argues that this spirit need not be collected and constructed from various works, but that it is already given in each individual work, since each work of antiquity is only an individualization of this spirit.[34] I do not contest that it is present in each text, but I doubt that it is recognizable without considerably more effort. We begin to see the difficulty if, in dealing with one of Demosthenes' speeches, I want to posit in addition to the spirit of antiquity the Hellenic spirit, and then also the spirit of Athenian oratorical eloquence, and then also the particular spirit of Demosthenes and, above all, the characteristics of the era and the special occasion of his speech, as the "body" to which it belongs. And if I add to this the observation that the spirit of antiquity is to be found not only in a certain type of written works but also in the graphic arts and who knows where else, this formula seems to break out of the specific limits of hermeneutics entirely, for hermeneutics deals only with what is produced in language. Ast's formula will surely fail to accomplish its goal.

If we reflect for only a moment on the procedure that some time ago was frequently based on just this statement, namely, the use of the technical language of one sphere in an entirely different sphere, then no one will deny that, even if such formulae are not a mere game founded on a sound view, they lead only to ruinous vagueness and indecision. Nor can I absolve Ast of these faults in the application of his theory. For when I read in this connection that the idea, as the unity which encompasses a life, both as its variety and form and as an absolute unity (the reverse would state the case better), then I find myself in a fog.[35] Such vagueness is not propitious for a theory that demands clarity. Everyone must grant that up to the point just described the level our interpretations have achieved is a notable step toward rightly conceiving the spirit of a people and of a time from the way language is used. Moreover, a theory developed from these observations receives substantial confirmation when studies in other areas of intellectual productivity yield similar results. But I do not wish a venture in the opposite direction and try to comprehend the

particular by such general hypotheses, nor do I wish to
suggest that such a procedure would still belong to hermeneutics.

This leads me to another point. Ast distinguishes
three kinds of understanding: historical, grammatical, and
an understanding of the spirit. To be precise, the understanding of spirit is itself twofold, directed toward both
the spirit of the individual author and the spirit of
classical antiquity as a whole. Thus he actually distinguishes four kinds of understanding. Taking his list of
three, however, he speaks of the third as the highest and
claims that it penetrates the other two.[36] It could
therefore be supposed that he actually intended to point
to the two stages of interpretation that we have disclosed
in exploring the formula that the particular can be understood only from the whole. But this supposition remains
at best highly uncertain. For if he considers the twofold
understanding of the spirit to be the higher one, and
grammatical and historical understanding to be the lower,
such that they occupy a single stage over against the understanding of the spirit and penetrated by it, why does
he not put them together and simply differentiate between
the lower and higher kinds of understanding? But the fact
of the matter is that he also speaks of a threefold hermeneutics, hermeneutics of the letter, of the sense, and of
the spirit, and this tripartite division is irreconcilable
with my supposition.[37] This distinction of a threefold
understanding of a threefold hermeneutics rests on the
fact that to him the understanding of speech is not the
same as interpretation, for interpretation is to him the
development of what has been understood.[38] This view, and
many have advocated it before Ast, only confuses the issue. By the term "development" he means nothing other
than the presentation of the genesis of understanding, the
communication of the way understanding has been attained.
Interpretation, then, is distinguished from understanding
only as articulated speech from internal speech, and some-

thing else would be introduced for the purpose of communication. Thus interpretation could occur only as the application of the general rules of eloquence without, however, adding anything to the contents or altering anything
in the text. Wolf also knows nothing about this matter
and defines hermeneutics as merely the art of discovering
the meaning of the text.[39] Were we to grant Ast his distinction, a threefold hermeneutics would follow only to
the extent that there would be that many ways of developing the understanding. But his instructions do not
point toward this, nor are they developed in this sense,
insofar as they are developed at all. Just as little,
however, do they agree with his three modes of understanding. Because the hermeneutics of the letter, which explains the words and content, deals with historical and
grammatical understanding, the hermeneutics of the sense
and the spirit are both included in the understanding of
the spirit. To be sure, this is twofold, but these two
hermeneutics cannot be distinguished in this way because
the one pertains exclusively to the spirit of the individual author and the other to the spirit of classical antiquity. The hermeneutics of sense deals only with the meaning [Bedeutung] of the letter in the context of a particular passage. On the other hand, both procedures offer an
explanation of the spirit in each passage, so in the end
nothing seems to harmonize.

This alone is clear: the explanation of words and
contents are not themselves interpretation but only elements of it, and hermeneutics begins with the determination of meaning, although to be sure by means of these
elements. Further, no explanation, that is, no determination of meaning, is correct unless it is supported by an
examination of the spirit of the author and the spirit of
classical antiquity. For only a person in a disturbed
state of mind speaks or writes against his own spirit,
and, were one to insist on an explanation of an ancient
writer that stands in clear contradiction to the spirit of

antiquity, one would have to prove that the author was a
mongrel in his spirit. Ast himself says as much when,
discussing the explanation of the sense, he argues that
whoever fails to grasp the spirit of an author is unable
to uncover the true meaning of particular passages and
that a proposed meaning is true only when it is in harmony
with that spirit.[40] Thus, although Ast divides his hermeneutics into three types, he actually offers us only a
single hermeneutics, the hermeneutics of the sense, because the hermeneutics of the letter is not yet hermeneutics and the hermeneutics of the spirit, insofar as it is
not encompassed by the hermeneutics of the sense, lies beyond the scope of hermeneutics altogether.

On this issue we must stand with Wolf, adding only
that in order to apply this technique fully to a text we
must not only explain the words and the content, but comprehend the spirit of the author as well. Wolf himself
admits as much, perhaps inadvertently, when he distinguishes interpretations into grammatical, historical, and
rhetorical.[41] By grammatical interpretation he means
the explanation of words, and by historical the explanation of the content. But he uses rhetorical in the same
sense as we use aesthetic today. Consequently, rhetorical
interpretation would in fact be hermeneutics only with
reference to the particular artistic genre, and it would
include only a portion of what Ast calls the understanding
of spirit, namely, those art-forms determined by the spirit of classical antiquity. In any case he would have had
to add a "poetic" interpretation to rhetorical in order to
exhaust what we mean by aesthetic. Consequently, were he
to attend also to the individual or special spirit of the
author, his hermeneutics would yield five different kinds
of interpretation. However correct this view may be, I
would have to protest against a formulation of the hermeneutical task that makes grammatical and historical interpretations seem to be special and distinct in themselves.
Theologians have already combined these two in order to

strengthen a good case against a bad one, and they make use of the phrase "grammatical-historical interpretation." Although in and of itself this is right, the phrase is used in opposition to dogmatic and allegorical interpretations, as if these represented independent types of interpretation, regardless of whether or not they are justified.[42]

Ast succumbs to a similar mistake when he distinguishes a simple meaning and an allegorical meaning, thereby leaving the impression that an allegorical meaning is a second and additional meaning.[43] But if a passage was intended to be allegorical, then the allegorical meaning is the only one and the simple one. The passage has no other meaning at all, and that meaning is understood historically. If a passage was intended to be allegorical, then by positing the allegorical meaning as a second one, the interpreter would not be reproducing the actual meaning of the words at all, because he would not be attributing to them the meaning they have in their context. And the reverse would be the case were he to give an allegorical explanation to a passage that was not intended to be taken allegorically. If the interpreter does this deliberately, he is no longer engaged in interpretation but in practical application; if he does it unintentionally, his explanation is simply false, and we have enough of those already--and they, by the way, are caused by this same mistake. One would be equally justified to invent a mystical interpretation for Masonic and other such formulae and then to distinguish the mysterious meaning from the simple one. Then, when we recall that some time ago a philosopher presented us with a moral meaning in addition to the dogmatic, for which the same conditions pertain as for the allegorical, we can only hope that the right position has been reached by the person who recently invented a panharmonic interpretation.[44] He surely intended nothing other than that in a correct interpretation all the various themes must concur in one and the same conclusion.

All these innovations seem to stem from the belief
that there are various kinds of interpretation from which
interpreters can freely choose. But were that so, it
would no longer be worth the effort to speak or write.
Unfortunately, it is abundantly clear that these various
interpretations have had a deleterious influence on hermeneutics. Since they grow out of the chaotic conditions of
the discipline, we may be sure they will not disappear until hermeneutics assumes the technical form it is due and,
starting from the simple fact of understanding by reference to the nature of language and to the fundamental conditions relating a writer and reader or a speaker and
hearer, develops its rules into a systematic, self-
contained discipline.

MANUSCRIPT 6

THE MARGINAL NOTES OF 1832-33

Notes to Manuscript 3

Hermeneutics. 1832, First Week 1-4.

Raising the task to the general standpoint. Begin with Ast and Wolf.[1] How hermeneutics and criticism are related, and how both in turn are related to grammar. Hermeneutics and grammar, however, also relate to rhetoric and dialectics. --That hermeneutics relates to both these areas is a feature it shares with all technical skills. --From this develop the two sides of the task, the linguistic and the personal. --Each side is carried to such an extent that at the end the result is the same as that reached by the other.

Second Week 5-9.

Neither task is higher or lower. --Both require a linguistic talent and knowledge of human nature. --The degree of significance which different texts hold for each task, according to 11. --The rules are to be regarded as "methods" for "recognizing" difficulties rather than as observations for overcoming them. --Concerning the relationship between general and specialized hermeneutics: grammatical, according to language, according to the distinction between poetry and prose; psychological, according to the genre. --Neither its language nor its genre requires that there be a special hermeneutics for the Bible, nor does its double layers of meaning. Does the

fact that it is inspired justify a special hermeneutics?
Investigate the maximum and minimum of this concept.
1832, Hour 10.

Inspiration, as an infusion into the mind [Gesin-
nung], should not influence the work of interpretation.[2]
If in the case of the Bible, as in every other case, the
goal of hermeneutics is to understand the texts as their
original readers understood them, the fact that they are
inspired does not affect the interpretation at all.
--Therefore, there is no special hermeneutics for the New
Testament because it is inspired, and the only remaining
possible justification for one is its complex use of language. (Note. Digress here to discuss juristic hermeneutics which, because of its special character, generally
extends beyond searching for what the author actually
thought to ask if the author would have included certain
cases, which had not arisen in his mind, under a given
rule.)
11. 12.

Even a special hermeneutics occasioned by both considerations is still related to general hermeneutics in
such a way that we could manage quite well with the general alone. The linguistic aspect of hermeneutics presupposes a knowledge of language as well as a knowledge of
the difference between prose and poetry. The personal aspect of hermeneutics presupposes the general experience of
states of mind and dispositions.

Before beginning, the interpreter must know what
weight is to be given each side in the application.
(12). The interpreter must then establish the same relationship between himself and the author as existed between
the author and his original audience. Therefore, the interpreter must be familiar with the whole sphere of life
and the relationships between author and audience. Without such complete knowledge, we encounter difficulties
which we had hoped to avoid. Commentaries anticipate and
try to resolve such difficulties. Whoever relies on them

is submitting to an authority, and in order to arrive at an independent understanding one must subject these authorities to one's own judgment.

13.

If a statement is addressed to me directly: But it must also be assumed that the speaker thinks of me just as I think of myself. Now since ordinary conversation provides ample evidence to demonstrate that this is not the case, we must proceed sceptically. Canon: The understanding we draw from the beginning of a text is to be confirmed by the rest. Thus it follows that our initial understanding must still be present when we arrive at our final one, and this means that statements which are too long to be retained by our normal powers of memory must be written down. This canon may now be stated as follows: "in order to understand the first part correctly, the whole must have already been understood."

1832, Continuation of 13.

Of course, this initial understanding is not equivalent to the sum of the particulars, but is like a skeleton or outline which can be formed by passing over the details. We follow this canon even when, beginning with this initial grasp, we proceed to reconstruct the process of the author, for authors of larger works always form an idea of the whole before they proceed to the details.

14.

In order to continue our train of thought without interruption we must investigate more closely what is to be avoided, namely, misunderstanding. A sentence may be quantitatively misunderstood when it is not grasped as a whole; it may be qualitatively misunderstood when irony is taken to be serious, and vice versa. The sentence, as a unity, is the smallest element which can be understood. Misunderstanding means to confuse one aspect of the linguistic value of a word or a form with another. This distinction between qualitative and quantitative misunderstanding, taken in its strict sense, runs throughout the

entire operation. Even the word "God" is subject to it, as are both the formal and material elements.
1832, Continuation of 14.

Misunderstanding arises in two ways, by not-understanding or directly. In the first instance it is possible that the author is at fault, but in the other it seems that the interpreter has only himself to blame. (See 17, Ms. 3). We could formulate the task of hermeneutics in negative terms: to avoid misunderstanding at every point. Since no one can be satisfied with outright not-understanding, it follows that when the task, as defined above, is correctly completed, full understanding has been attained. Once the task has been understood and the pre-conditions for its initiation have been met, priority must be given to one of the two sides. The grammatical side deserves priority, both because it is the most highly developed and because in it previous works on the subject can most readily be taken into account.

1832, Hour 15. Grammatical Interpretation

First Canon. The common area of language is the act of using language.
Hour 16.

Explain 1,3,4,a,b. And concerning new words. The necessity of recognizing their importance, especially when a topic is treated for the first time.
Hour 17.

New words are not in fact exceptions to the rule since their meaning must always be understood in terms of the context in which they appear.

Condition for undisturbed progress in a sentence is the complete determinability of each element in terms of all others. If this condition cannot be met, it is necessary to consult a lexicon. Two types of lexica, alphabetical and etymological.
18.

Discuss antitheses and changes of meaning. Such expressions as <u>coma arborum</u> are not figurative. To trans-

late this expression as "leaves" is a quantitative misunderstanding.[3]
19.

     Therefore, there are no figurative meanings at all,
or not as antithetical meanings. To be sure, the unity of
a word is not always the same; later discoveries could
have been made, or concepts could have arisen which extend
the meaning. Consequently, the interpreter must know not
only that a given meaning is characteristic of an author's style, but also whether this meaning originated
with him or was already in current use. Otherwise quantitative misunderstanding results.
25.

     Having shown how the principle of the context can be
extended, it was noted that it must be modified for leading thoughts, for secondary thoughts and for thoughts
which are merely means of representation [Darstellungsmit-
tel]. These distinctions are always sharpest in works
governed by a logical train of thought. At the one extreme is lyrical poetry, where the thought is only a means
of representation, and at the other extreme systematic,
scientific texts, where everything is a main thought and
each detail is only a part. In the former instance the
interpreter must begin to deal with the details right
away; in the latter he must attempt to understand as much
as possible all at once.
26.

     Gradation between these extremes: the epistolary
form is nearest the lyrical; the historical form nearest
the systematic; and the didactic, since it can also be
rhetorical, represents the mean.

     In order to explain leading thoughts the interpreter
should consider them within a sphere comprising the identity of two entire complexes. Parenthetical remarks do
not affect the construction of this sphere. Similar complexes may be found in other works. At each point the interpreter must be certain that the use of language is

identical, because often the differences are subtle. --In order to explain secondary thoughts the interpreter should use only similar passages with truly parallel leading thoughts, seeking to ascertain their overall value as well as their degree of similarity. At the same time, however, the interpreter must note how evident the psychological facts are in this author.

27.

Explanations made by reference to antitheses are analogous to understanding the part in terms of the whole. But some concepts shade off into each other (especially nouns, the latter especially from verbs).

28.

The more difficult transitions. The entire circle must be kept in mind, and explanations can be drawn only from an author who uses these same members of the circle.

On thoughts which are only means of representation. The general type is comparison: the extremes are fully developed allegories and simple metaphorical expressions. Some are unscientific; others, arbitrary. In the latter instance the tertium comparationis cannot be found unless the interpreter is acquainted with the variety and development of the subject matter. (Many instances of these in Jean Paul. Difficulties which could have been avoided in Hamann.)

29.

Even arbitrary comparisons, if they contain any truth at all, must be able to be traced back to a decisive analogy. When this analogy is too obscure, so that the comparison is used as an actual part of the description (as in Hamann), the author is difficult.

Interrupt here in order to apply these rules to the New Testament. It is difficult to determine the identity of the context for the epistolary form, and it is difficult, too, for the historical form, since they could be compilations. Therefore, passages which do not belong to the same narrative are to be treated as though they were written by another author.

The chief question, that is, to what extent the New Testament is a whole, will be directed first to John. 30.

In order to answer this question, refer to what was said above. But, considered as a collection, the New Testament must be referred back to our general principles. (a) A collection of writings by one author dealing with different topics is unified only by the author's individual treatment of language. (b) Writings by different authors dealing with the same topic need to be contrasted, inasmuch as they differ from each other. If the authors were not acquainted with each other, the interpreter must be very cautious in his use of them. 1832, Continuation of 30.

This consideration applies in large measure to the New Testament. The speeches of Christ are similar to these.

Warn against hastily extracting passages from their context. 31.

Examples of simple determinations of subject and predicate in the New Testament found in simple sentences and their immediate contexts.

a. John 7:39 See John 14 and 16 passim, where both οὔπω εἶναι and πνεῦμα occur. Moreover, John could not have reflected upon the Old Testament usage, as the οὔπω ἦν shows, for otherwise he would have had to say "the spirit was not yet again there."

b. I Corinthians 15:31, the θηριουμάχομαι can represent only a particular case for καθ᾽ ἡμέραν ἀνασθνήσκω.

c. Matthew 5:44, 16 φῶς from καλὰ ἔργα. Compare Ephesians 5:8.

32.

Detailed examples. John 8:28 and 12:32. John wants
in verse 33 only to suggest an allusion; the proper meaning is related to κρίσις τοῦ κόσμου and ὑψωθεὶς ἑλκύσω
is in opposition to ἄρχων ἐκβληθήσεται. Both instances of
κρισὶς τοῦ κόσμου as well as the repeated ἀσυνδέκος signify νῦν (compare Dittman, p. 459).[4] It would seem that the
former passage, 8:28, refers exclusively to the death, because in it an activity is attributed to the Jews and because, understood spiritually, it seems that the knowledge
must precede the ὑψώσητε.[5] But

1. All of the material that follows belongs to the
γνώσεσθε, and the subjective "lifting up" must precede this knowledge, for no doubt this activity can
also be attributed to them. However, understood
from the conclusion (if ὅταν also remains uncer-
tain--as an example of ὅταν and τότε where the latter governs, the author cites Plato, p. 436) Christ
would have to have said: "when you kill me you will
believe."

2. Christ had previously said that if they would
not believe they would die in their sins, and to
this is added in the form of a contrast: "but when
you lift him up you will reach this knowledge." The
parallel passage 3:14 treats the "lifting up" [of
the serpent] as a sign.

33.

Examples of explaining from antitheses, as in 13.

34.

General explanation of the formal element.

Notes to Manuscript 4

Winter Semester 1832-33.
1833, January 3. 44th Hour.

Recapitulate the relative distinction between psychological and technical interpretation. The former

focuses more upon how thoughts emerged from the totality of the author's life. The latter focuses more upon how a set of thoughts arose from a particular thought or intention [Darstellenwollen]. The two procedures are closest when an author stuck to his original decision and avoided all incidental interests. As a rule technical interpretation seeks to understand the meditation and composition. Psychological interpretation seeks to understand the creative ideas, including those fundamental thoughts which gave rise to the entire train of thought and the secondary thoughts. Psychological interpretation consists of two parts. Psychological interpretation is easier and more certain when the interpreter and the author combine thoughts in the same way and when the interpreter has a detailed knowledge of the author's thoughts.
45.

Meditation and composition are always two distinct activities. Sometimes meditation can focus on a decision in such a static way that it is only incidentally effective, and of course in such cases the composition is clearly a second, distinct act. But in the final analysis the two are always distinct. Even though the initial decision predetermines what the form will be, including many of its exceptions and positive determinations, the composition may evolve in such a way that this original decision must be temporarily set aside.
46.

This division into two parts makes it difficult to decide whether the major organizational divisions are to be retained or the subordinate divisions are to be treated in the order of their composition. Discover the author's decision, i.e., the unity and actual direction of the work (psychological); then, understand the composition as the objective realization of that decision; and, then, understand the meditation as the genetic realization (these latter two, technical). Then, discover the secondary

thoughts as the on-going influence of the totality of
life.

We do, however, want to retain the major organizational divisions, and, although we naturally begin by understanding the impulse, we proceed to consider how the
totality of life affected the development of the whole.
In proceeding in this way, we can assume that any part of
the composition which is mentioned must be already known
from the literary life.

1833, Continuation of 46.

Of course, it might be supposed that the title of
the work is sufficient to resolve our first task. But
that is a mistake. Titles are by no means essential, and
in antiquity they were almost always omitted. Moreover,
they may be completely accidental, e.g., the Iliad, where
the title does not indicate anything about the work.

The resolution of the task of finding the unity of
the work is confined to the area between two extremes:
when the unity is self-evident and when it is impossible
to identify.

47.

The essential difference between a work in which the
unity is self-evident and one in which the unity is impossible to identify is that the form of the work, insofar as
it is already established, is dictated by the original decision about its composition. Consequently, the author is
understood to be an organ of this form, as one part of his
intellectual life, just as in grammatical interpretation
he is understood to be an organ of language. Even an inventor of a form is to be regarded in these terms. For
this new form, too, must have a basis in life, and so this
external basis directs the author.

Psychological Part

First task: To find the unity of a work as a deed of
the author. If the form of a work is dictated by the author's profession, the answer to the general question

about its relation to his life is obvious, and it needs
only to be made specific.
48.

There is a difference between asking "under what
circumstances did the author come to his original decision" and asking "what did this decision mean to him."
Since the former question is concerned merely with external matters, it leads to answers that deal merely with ex-
ternals. That which was once present in the mind [Gemüth]
and life of an author will come to expression along with
other ideas in life.

The second question is far more important. When a
work is dictated by an author's profession, the general
answer is usually obvious, and only the specific cause remains to be found. The question becomes more difficult,
however, when the work is a matter of indifference to the
author. Only in the case of true works of art does the
question of the relationship of content and form come into
consideration. The hermeneutical task must be resolved,
however, in the case of many works dominated by a single
purpose.
49.

In such cases an author frequently tries to conceal
his purpose among a variety of topics, and even though his
contemporaries may have been aware of this purpose, later
readers may consider him to be ambiguous. Consequently,
the interpreter should first identify the unity of the
work from the details, and of course by reference to the
composition of the work, insofar as that has been understood. Discuss how the purpose of a work is concealed by
referring to the hypothesis of an anti-Christian tendency
in such a work as Gibbon's.[6]
50.

The hidden unity can be found in passages where the
details have not been totally connected into the unity of
content and form, and where this unconnected material has
a common point of reference.

An original decision may be related to an author's life in
one of three ways, leading him to write: a book (the maximum here is when he works on the book throughout the
course of his life); an occasional piece (the minimum here
is when it is not related at all to his profession but is
purely incidental); studies, as exercises for works, usually ranging from occasional pieces to works.
51-55.

Since this classification applies only to truly artistic works, it is applicable to scientific works only to
the extent that they are artistic. It applies to other
works only when there are no purely didactic purposes concealed in them. Moreover, the unity of the original decision may be stronger or weaker. It is weakest when the
author's decision was simply to indulge himself in expressing his thoughts. In this case the distinction between
major and secondary thoughts simply disappears, with the
result that each thought must be considered independently.
But this lack of coherence may be merely apparent, or the
connection may have been intentionally concealed. If so,
it can be recognized only by following the general rule
(50).

Application to New Testament Hermeneutics. We will
omit the Apocalypse at the outset and concern ourselves
only with the historical and epistolary forms. We first
discuss the historical forms, starting of course with the
four books which recount the life of Jesus. In all four
the continuity of the passion story is in obvious contrast
to the fragmentary narrative of the earlier parts. Yet
this contrast is less pronounced in John than in the first
three. The gospels differ in that some begin with the
birth of Jesus, others with his public ministry. Does
this difference presuppose another basic unity? Yes,
1833, 51-55.
if the birth is excluded because it does not fit into the
plan of the work or if it is included because it tells of
the miraculous aspect of Jesus' life. No, if the birth

was omitted because the authors noted its congruity with
the later cultus and if the public ministry was included
because they did not want to leave anything out.

The synoptics treat the earlier sections of the work
differently than John, in that John provides absolute,
precise time references, whereas the other three are more
vague. The later narratives are not structured in accord
with a biographical idea, but are unified only in the
sense that the authors tried to collect all the details.
Thus in the first three as well as in John we must raise
the question as to their points of view.

When we attempt to offer an equally comprehensive
treatment of the epistolary form, we note the possibility
that it approximates a strict form. But it is also possible that the epistles were written freely, without form.
This latter possibility can in turn be treated by reference to the writers' points of view or by reference to the
situation within which they wrote. These two considerations can also be combined, sometimes rather loosely, at
other times quite tightly. Likewise, these two main forms
can be connected to each other, in part to bring into focus the intermediary form between them.
56-59.

A digression may be defined as a freely-written narrative found between two particular points.

AFTERWORD OF 1968
by Heinz Kimmerle

In response to my edition of F. D. E. Schleiermacher's manuscripts on hermeneutics, published in 1959 by
the Carl Winter Verlag in Heidelberg, numerous supplements, critical views, and questions of interpretation
have been advanced which deserve to be summarized and ex-
amined critically. Such a summary is also in order because these comments have come from philosophical as well
as theological circles and as a result not all of the comments are readily available to both disciplines.

My edition was the first publication of some of
these manuscripts, and a historically-critically edited
text could not be offered. In the course of research for
my dissertation "Die Hermeneutik Schleiermachers im Zusammenhang seines spekulativen Denkens" (Heidelberg, 1957), I
observed that in his edition of Hermeneutik und Kritik,
published as volume 7 of part 1 of Schleiermacher's collected works, Lücke had evidently not taken Schleiermacher's early manuscripts into consideration, but had
sought to reproduce the final, most mature form of
Schleiermacher's thought. At that time I suspected that
these early manuscripts contained fruitful statements
which were not later developed or which were for other
reasons covered over. This opinion was confirmed by an
examination of these manuscripts in the Literaturarchiv of
the German Academy of Sciences in Berlin. Thus my edition
made these important but previously unpublished handwritten manuscripts available for the first time, and it be-

came possible to view the entire span of development of Schleiermacher's thought on hermeneutics, from his first notes to the lecture manuscripts dating from the last years of his life.

The older edition in the collected works has not, however, become superfluous, since Lücke used, in addition to manuscript materials, sections from student lecture notes which he incorporated into the text.[1] This part of his edition will be definitely superseded only by the preparation of a historical-critical edition in which the significance of these newly published materials would for the first time become clear.

The publication of these manuscripts was met with lively attention. The new texts were compared with those already known and their meaning was evaluated. I refer in particular to the discussions by W. Pannenberg in Monatsschrift für Pastoraltheolgie 49 (1960): 444ff.; H. G. Geyer in Zeitschrift für Kirchengeschichte 72 (1961): 197ff.; Christoph Senft in Philosophische Rundchau 10 (1962): 288ff.; and H. J. Birkner in Verkündigung und Forschung (1962): 150ff. In his review Geyer traced the development of Schleiermacher's thoughts on hermeneutics by reference to all of these manuscripts and discussed their import for the contemporary debate on hermeneutics. Geyer sought to show that "in Schleiermacher a progressive dissolution of the connection between language and the process of understanding is related to an increasing emphasis on the connection between language and subjective consciousness." Geyer suggests that "perhaps the aporie with which the contemporary hermeneutical discussion is burdened results from that covering of spirit which is reflected in the development of Schleiermacher's thought on hermeneutics, and from its psychological and historical, and thus radically subjectivistic, consequences." But Geyer has failed to demonstrate clearly enough how a consideration of these early manuscripts may somehow provide a dimension in which the present aporie may be overcome.

Since the publication of these manuscripts, several comments on the interpretation of Schleiermacher's hermeneutics have been made. H. G. Gadamer referred to my new edition in his exposition of Schleiermacher in his book Wahrheit und Methode.[2] But Schleiermacher remains for him the exponent of "the questionableness of romantic hermeneutics." The attempt he makes in his second edition to define the correct meaning of Schleiermacher's development as a withdrawal from an (originally living) grammatical-rhetorical to a psychological tradition did not lead him to regard Schleiermacher's early conception of understanding as purely linguistical understanding and his conception of history as the history of language to be of positive value for his own problematic.[3] Had he done so, Schleiermacher's theories could have been of direct benefit, especially in the conclusion of his book where language is considered as "[the universal] medium of hermeneutical experience."

In his review W. Pannenberg attempts to demonstrate that the late form of Schleiermacher's thoughts represents the "logical development" of his original position. "For the fact that a specific expression is understood as an empirical modification of an ideal reality is already raised as a problem in the early distinction between the general meaning of a world and its particular nuances. This problem . . . is later resolved by psychological construction."[4] But does not this distinction involve other essential moments as well? Does the psychological moment somehow stand already in the foreground?

Recently, in the Introduction of his edition of part 2 of Dilthey's Leben Schleiermachers, Martin Redeker contests the history of the development of Schleiermacher's hermeneutics which I had set forth in my edition of the Hermeneutics.[5] He attempts to show that Dilthey's view of Schleiermacher--which should be corrected in light of these newly published handwritten manuscripts--is correct. Since throughout his edition Redeker accepts

Dilthey's manuscripts too uncritically and values them too highly as direct contributions for further research on Schleiermacher, he also makes a relatively uncritical identification of Dilthey's views with Schleiermacher's late position on hermeneutics. To be sure, it is completely correct to note that the "concept of psychology," as "Schleiermacher and even Dilthey had used the term," did not mean what it means today. Yet the decisive break--and Dilthey himself was unaware of it--occurred between Schleiermacher and Dilthey. Consequently, the later views of Schleiermacher on the "double process of psychologizing and historicizing which was passed on to the thinking of the nineteenth century" are to be deemphasized and understood in terms of the early conception, the fruitfulness of which for an objective explanation of the problem has not yet been rightly considered.[6]

In several shorter studies I have proceeded from a grasp of the notion of individuality as the systematic kernel of Schleiermacher's philosophy and sought to show the significance of his early drafts on hermeneutics for the current philosophical-hermeneutical problematic.[7] This attempt takes on a new theoretical and practical aspect when one seeks to grasp the problem of the understanding of meaning in terms of its concrete social context. Schleiermacher shows that the ethical process, in his sense of the term, that is, cultural and social-political development as a whole, is carried on by individualities, not only those of particular persons, but also those of intersubjective individualities, cultural-social-political unities of action which possess characteristic, determinate linguistic forms or linguistic possibilities. Thus the work of the historical and humane sciences assumes a central meaning for society as a whole, in that they are to appropriate past history in an understanding way for the present.

Hermann Patsch has published a study entitled "On the Early History of Romantic Hermeneutics."[8] This work

represents an important deepening and differentiation of
our understanding of Schleiermacher, so that his profundity and relevance becomes far more clear. Josef Körner,
who had published Friedrich Schlegel's fragments On
Philology of 1797 as the "meagre remains" of his Drafts
for a Philosophy of Philology, had considered Schleiermacher's hermeneutics only "in their original dependence
upon Schlegel."[9] Patsch, on the other hand, finds in the
time of Schlegel and Schleiermacher's stay in Berlin
(1797-98) the common roots for the related thoughts in the
theoretical works of the two men, and he has attempted to
trace Schleiermacher's own development. Consequently, the
thesis of direct dependence is modified to state that "in
Schlegel much is prefigured that Schleiermacher later sys-
tematized and developed."[10] Nonetheless, this method of
inquiry, too, overlooks the fact that Schleiermacher's
early thoughts on the philosophy of language, in which the
special significance of his conceptions of hermeneutics is
found, have no parallel in Schlegel.

Our knowledge of Dilthey's interpretation of
Schleiermacher's hermeneutics is substantially expanded by
Redeker's publication of Dilthey's prize-winning essay Das
eigentümliche Verdienst der Schleiermacherschen Hermeneutik ist durch Vergleichung mit älteren Bearbeitungen
dieser Schrift, namentlich von Ernesti and Keil, ins Licht
zu setzen."[11] The revision of this essay, for which the
Schleiermacher-Stiftung awarded Dilthey twice the usual
honorarium in 1860, had previously been available only in
the form of an abstract.[12] It shows that Dilthey knew of
and sought to utilize Schleiermacher's early aphorisms
(1805 and 1809-10). In this essay the grammatical part of
hermeneutics is given far more attention than in Dilthey's
later short essay of 1900 "The Origin of Hermeneutics."[13]
Unfortunately, Dilthey did not have access to the so-
called "First Draft" of Schleiermacher's hermeneutics
(1809-10), where grammatical understanding is founded in
the philosophy of language. Consequently, he could only

conclude about the aphorisms that "as fine as these remarks are, it is still not possible to see in them a basic,
coherent view of the nature of language."[14] Dilthey's interpretation of the early aphorisms was determined primarily by the view he gained from Lücke's edition which, as
he knew, reflected by and large the "final period" of
Schleiermacher's development. "The aphorisms," Dilthey
states, "present to us . . . the impelling thought from
which his hermeneutics developed: the essence of interpretation is the reconstruction of the work as a living act
of the author."[15]

NOTES

TRANSLATORS' INTRODUCTION

1. Wilhelm Dilthey, "Die Entstehung der Hermeneutik," in Gesammelte Schriften, ed. Georg Misch, vol. 5: Die geistige Welt: Einleitung in die Philosophie des Lebens (Stuttgart: B. G. Tübner, 1924), pp. 327, 329, 333; Die Religion in Geschichte und Gegenwart, 3d ed., s. v. "Hermeneutik," by Gerhard Ebeling; and Joachim Wach, Das Verstehen: Grundzüge einer Geschichte der hermeneutischen Theorie im 19. Jahrhundert, 3 vols. in 1 (Hildesheim: Georg Olms, 1966), 1: 85-86. The best introduction to the history of modern hermeneutics available in English is Richard Palmer, Hermeneutics: Interpretation Theory in Schleiermacher, Dilthey, Heidegger, and Gadamer (Evanston, Illinois: Northwestern University Press, 1969). An important interpretation of eighteenth and nineteenth century hermeneutical theory is to be found in Hans Frei, The Eclipse of Biblical Narrative (New Haven and London: Yale University Press, 1974).

2. Friedrich Schleiermacher, Sämmtliche Werke, pt. 1, vol. 7: Hermeneutik und Kritik mit besonderer beziehung auf das Neue Testament, ed. Friedrich Lücke (Berlin: G. Reimer, 1838).

3. Ms. 3, pp. 109-10.

4. Ms. 3, pp. 148-49.

5. Ms. 6, pp. 223-24.

6. The significance of the hermeneutical circle is emphasized by Dilthey, "Die Entstehung der Hermeneutik," p. 330; Palmer, Hermeneutics, pp. 87-88; and Wach, Das Verstehen, 1: 41-43. The hermeneutical circle has been reconceived by Hans-Georg Gadamer, Wahrheit und Methode: Grundzüge einer philosophischen Hermeneutik, 3d ed. rev. (Tübingen: J. C. B. Mohr [Paul Siebeck], 1972), pp. 250-90; English trans. of the 2d ed.: Truth and Method, ed. Garrett Barden and John Cumming (New York: Seabury Press, 1975), pp. 235-74.

7. The image of "suspension" is discussed by H. Jackson Forstman, "The Understanding of Language by

Friedrich Schlegel and Schleiermacher," Soundings 51
(1968): 156-58.

8. Ms. 1, p. 50.

9. The chief contest in philosophical hermeneutics
is that between Gadamer, Wahrheit und Methode and Emilio
Betti, Allgemeine Auslegungslehre als Methodik der
Geisteswissenschaften (Tübingen: J. C. B. Mohr [Paul
Siebeck], 1967. See Palmer, Hermeneutics, pp. 46-65. In
theology the debate issued in proposals for a "new herme-
neutic" discussed at length in James M. Robinson and John
B. Cobb, Jr., eds. The New Hermeneutic, New Frontiers in
Theology, vol. 2 (New York: Harper and Row, 1964).

10. The summary is from Kimmerle's Introduction to
his edition, pp. 27-40 above.

11. Dilthey, "Die Entstehung der Hermeneutik," and
Gadamer, Wahrheit und Methode, p. 162.

12. See pp. 30-31 above.

13. See p. 31 above, as well as Kimmerle's "Afterword of 1968," pp. 232-33 above.

14. See pp. 229-34 above. A thoughtful critique of
Kimmerle's interpretation of Schleiermacher's development
is offered by John Edward Benson, "Schleiermacher's Hermeneutics" (Ph.D. dissertation, Columbia University, 1967),
pp. 392-407.

15. This question, in slightly different guise, was
raised by Richard Palmer and James Edie in response to
Hans-Georg Gadamer's article, "The Problem of Language in
Schleiermacher's Hermeneutics," trans. David Linge, in
Journal for Theology and the Church, vol. 6: Schleier-
macher as Contemporary, ed. Robert W. Funk (New York:
Herder and Herder, 1970), pp. 88-90, 93.

16. The increasing influence of linguistics on hermeneutical discussions raises this question forcefully.
See, for example, Paul Ricoeur, "Structure, Word, Event,"
trans. Robert D. Sweeny, Philosophy Today 12 (1968): 62-
75.

17. The importance of Schlegel for Schleiermacher's
conception of hermeneutics is emphasized by Hermann
Patsch, "Friedrich Schlegels 'Philosophie der Philologie'
und Schleiermachers Frühe Entwürfe zur Hermeneutik: Zur
Frühgeschichte der romantischen Hermeneutik," Zeitschrift
für Theologie und Kirche 63 (1966): 434-72 [hereafter referred to as "Zur Frühgeschichte der romantischen Hermeneutik"]. In "The Understanding of Language in Friedrich
Schlegel and Schleiermacher," H. Jackson Forstman has attempted a judicious reappraisal of the relationship between Schlegel and Schleiermacher.

18. See Paul Ricoeur, <u>Interpretation Theory: Discourse and the Surplus of Meaning</u> (Fort Worth, Texas: Texas Christian University Press, 1976), p. 93.

19. See Kimmerle's Introduction, pp. 21-27 above and nn. 5-15 cited there.

EDITOR'S INTRODUCTION

1. Schleiermacher, <u>Sämmtliche Werke</u>, pt. 1, vol. 7.

2. Ibid., p. vii.

3. Ibid., p. 8, n. 1; reference is made to Schleiermacher, <u>Sämmtliche Werke</u>, pt. 3, vol. 3: <u>Reden und Abhandlungen der Königlichen Akademie der Wissenschaftlichen vorgetragen.</u>

4. F. D. E. Schleiermacher, <u>Werke: Auswahl in vier Bändern</u>, ed. Otto Braun and D. J. Bauer, vol. 2: <u>Entwürfe zu einem System der Sittenlehre</u> (Leipzig: Felix Meiner, 1911).

5. TRANS.: In his "Afterword of 1968" Kimmerle retitles this manuscript as Manuscript 1: The Aphorisms of 1805 and 1809-10, with a loose page without date (Ms. 1').

6. TRANS.: In his "Afterword of 1968" Kimmerle retitles this manuscript as Manuscript 2: The First Draft of 1809-10, with a loose page from 1810-11 (Ms. 2').

7. TRANS.: In his "Afterword of 1968" Kimmerle notes that Patsch, "<u>Zur Frühgeschichte der romantischen Hermeneutik</u>," dates this manuscript in the winter of 1810, but Kimmerle finds the evidence for this dating to be insufficient.

8. TRANS.: In his "Afterword of 1968" Kimmerle accepts Patsch's judgment that Ms. 2" is a draft dating from 1822. It is, therefore, placed after Ms. 3 and retitled as Manuscript 3': A Draft for the Presentation of the Second Part--Application of Knowledge about the Author's Distinctiveness to Interpretation.

9. TRANS.: The full title of this portion of the text is now the Compendium of 1819 with Marginal Notes of 1828 (Ms. 3) and a Draft for the Presentation of the Second Part, 1822 (Ms. 3').

10. F. D. E. Schleiermacher, <u>Kurze Darstellung der theologischen Studiums zum Behuf einleitender Vorlesungen</u>, ed. Heinrich Scholz (Leipzig: A. Deichert, 1910; reprint ed. Hildesheim: G. Olms, 1961). English trans.: <u>Brief Outline of the Study of Theology</u>, trans. Terence N. Tice (Richmond: John Knox Press, 1966).

11. TRANS.: The Marginal Notes of 1828 have been included in this edition as footnotes to the text of Ms. 3.

12. TRANS.: The Marginal Notes of 1832-33 have been included in this edition as Ms. 6.

13.   TRANS.: In his "Afterword of 1968" Kimmerle
notes that this manuscript probably dates from the winter
semester, 1826-27.   The word Darstellung has been rendered
as "Exposition" in order to distinguish this manuscript
from Ms. 3'.

14.   TRANS.: These notes have been omitted in the
translation.

15.   TRANS.: Kimmerle's remarks on the reconstruction
of the text should be compared with the translators' remarks on the text and translation, pp. 15-18 above.

16.   Schleiermacher, Sämmtliche Werke, pt. 1, vol. 7,
p. viii.

17.   Ibid., pt. 3, vol. 3, pp. 294-95.

18.   Dilthey, "Die Entstehung der Hermeneutik," pp.
317ff.

19.   Rudolf Odebrecht, Introduction to Dialektik, by
F. D. E. Schleiermacher (Leipzig: J. C. Hinrichs, 1942),
p. xxiii.

20.   Budolf Bultmann, "Das Problem der Hermeneutik,"
in Glauben und Verstehen (Tübingen: J. C. B. Mohr [Paul
Siebeck], 1952), 2: 211-35; English trans.: "The Problem
of Hermeneutics," in Essays Philosophical and Theological,
trans. J. C. G. Grieg (London: SCM, 1955), pp. 234-62.

21.   Dilthey, "Die Entstehung der Hermeneutik,"
p. 327.

22.   Heinz Kimmerle, Die Hermeneutik Schleiermachers
im Zusammenhang seines spekulativen Denkens (Heidelberg,
1957).   TRANS.: Kimmerle has also written several articles
dealing with Schleiermacher's hermeneutics: "Hermeneutische Theorie oder ontologische Hermeneutik," Zeitschrift
für Theologie und Kirche 59 (1962): 114-30 ["Hermeneutical
Theory or Ontological Hermeneutics," trans. Friedrich
Seifert, in Journal for Theology and the Church, 6: 107-
21]; "Metahermeneutik, Applikation, hermeneutische
Sprachbildung," Zeitschrift für Theologie und Kirche 61
(1964): 221-35; Sprachfähigkeit und Weltbewaltigung,"
Philosophisches Jahrbuch 73 (1965-66): 356-71; and "Das
Verhältnis Schleiermachers zum Transcendental Idealismus,"
Kant Studien 51 (1959-60): 410-26.

23.   Kimmerle refers to Schleiermacher's Kurze
Darstellung des theologischen Studiums, p. 54.

24.   Ibid., pp. 54-55.   See also Ms. 6, pp. 215-17
above.

25.   Schleiermacher, Sämmtliche Werke, pt. 3, vol. 1,
p. 4.

26.   Schleiermacher, Werke: Auswahl, vol. 2.

27.   TRANS.: Kimmerle had originally entitled this
Ms. 2", but it is now cited as Ms. 3', p. 153 above.

28.   Schleiermacher, Werke: Auswahl 2: 97.

29.   This reference is now found in Ms. 3', p. 154 above.

30.   Schleiermacher, Kurze Darstellung des theologischen Studiums, p. 53.

31.   Schleiermacher, Werke: Auswahl; 2: 550.

32.   Schleiermacher, Sämmtliche Werke, pt. 3, vol. 2, p. 232.

33.   Ibid., pt. 1, vol. 8, p. 7.

MANUSCRIPTS 1 AND 1'

1.   Here and in numerous places in the text Schleiermacher refers to Johann August Ernesti, Institutio Interpretis Novi Testamenti, 1st ed. (Leipzig, 1761).

2.   Ernesti divides the first part of his book, which deals with subtilitas intelligendi, into two chief sections: Section 1. Contemplativa and Section 2. Praeceptiva. The second part deals with subtilitas explicandi, which Schleiermacher does not include in hermeneutics. The third part deals with various aids and solutions for hermeneutics. See Aphorism 1, p. 41 above.

3.   Against Ernesti, Institutio, Prol., §5.

4.   Cf. Ibid., §6. Schleiermacher's reference to the expression "an aliquid praeter verbum cogitemus" occurs for the first time in the third edition of Ernesti's Institutio (Leipzig, 1775). Consequently, Schleiermacher did not use the first edition cited in n. 1 above, or the second edition (Leipzig, 1765), but the third, or the fourth edition, edited by Ammon (Leipzig, 1792).

5.   The contents of the sections refer again to Ernesti, Institutio, Prol. TRANS.: A textual correction has been noted.

6.   Schleiermacher refers to Samuel F. N. Morus, Super hermeneutica Novi Testamenti acroases academicae, ed. Eichstaëdt (Leipzig, 1707). Other references to this work are made in the text. In this work (vol. 1, pp. 16-17) the terms usus loquendi and parallelismus are introduced as "principia vero exegetica . . . , de quibus convenit inter omnes eos, qui libros interpretantur."

7.   Morus reads Romans 14:23 as πᾶν δὲ ὃ οὐκ ἐκ πίστεως ἁμαρτία ἐστίν, and he interprets it by the statement "if one does not act from conviction, one can easily commit sin." TRANS.: A textual correction has been noted.

8.   See Ernesti, Institutio, pt. I, sec. 1, chap. 1, §§4-5. Schleiermacher argues against the distinction between a single sense (sensus) [Sinn] and several possible meanings (significationes) [Bedeutungen].

9. The distinction among different senses [Sinnen]
has played an important role in the history of hermeneutics. Ernesti attempts (Institutio, pt. I, sec. 1, chap.
1, §§7-11) to trace the different senses back to the literal one (sensus literalis) as the grammatical sense
(sensus grammaticus).

10. Ernesti, Institutio, pt. I, sec. 1, chap. 1,
§§1-11, esp. §§4-5.

11. Cf. Friedrich Schlegel's Lucinde (Berlin, 1799);
Ludwig Tieck's Romantische Dichtungen, 2 vols. (Jena,
1799-1800). See the reference noted by Patsch, "Zur
Frühgeschichte der romantischen Hermeneutik, p. 442, n.
36.

12. The Latin examples come from Morus, Super hermeneutica, 1: 260-61.

13. Ibid., pp. 260-62. In order to explain figurative meanings, Morus introduces similitudo and coniunctio.
He distinguishes further between the coniunctio rei
sensibilis and coniuctio rei intelligibilis. TRANS.: A
textual correction has been noted.

14. Ibid., p. 260; the example is given there.

15. Cf. G. L. Spalding, Vorrede zu Platonis Dialogi
quatuor (Platonis Dialogi selecti, vol. 1), ed. L. F.
Heindorf (Berlin: 1802), pp. v-viii, esp. pp. vi-vii.

16. In Super hermeneutica Morus distinguishes as
different types [Gattungen] which are to be considered in
explaining figurative expressions: (1) laws (1: 281-82),
(2) narratives (1: 282-90), and (3) dogmatic loci (1: 290-
91).

17. Cf. the section entitled "In allegorico loco
consulenda historia est" in Morus, Super hermeneutica, 1:
311-12. On p. 212 Morus cites Jn. 21:18-19 as an example,
where it predicts the death Peter will die. In the next
section, p. 313, Morus cites Lk. 5:36 as an example: "No
one sews an old patch on a new dress." TRANS.: A textual
correction has been noted.

18. See Platonis Dialogi selecti, ed. L. F. Heindorf, vol. (Berlin, 1802), p. 105 and vol. 2 (Berlin:
1805), p. 208. The explanation of ὅ, τι μαθών is first
found in the third volume, which appeared in Berlin in
1806, although it is possible that it was available at the
end of 1805. This latter detail is proof that the Aphorisms come from this period. TRANS.: A textual correction
has been noted.

19. Cf. Ernesti, Institutio, pt. 1, sec. 1, chap. 2,
§17 and Morus, Super hermeneutica, 1: 323-25. The word
audivi is found in the section on emphases temporariae
(Morus, p. 323); urbs is used as an example in the preceeding section (p. 321).

20. Cf. Morus, Super hermeneutica, 1: 324, summus wir mit Namen. TRANS.: A textual correction has been noted.

21. Schleiermacher is referring to Kant's statement that, in response to King Friedrich Wilhelm's objection to his work Die Religion innerhalb der Grenzen der blossen Vernunft (Königsberg, 1793-94), he declared himself "a loyal subject of his eternal Royal Highness" and promised to refrain from "further public statements on religion." Yet in the Foreword to Der Streit der Fakultäten (1798), written after the death of the King, Kant emphasized: "I made this statement carefully, so that I would not renounce my freedom of judgment on religious matters forever, but only as long as the King was alive."

22. The example is from Mt. 13:25.

23. Cf. Morus, Super hermeneutica, 1: 149-60, Orationis contextus patens, a) e scopo scriptoris; Ernesti, Institutio, pt. I, sec. 2, chap. 1, §§2-3.

24. August Wilhelm Schlegel, Gedichte (Tübingen, 1800). On p. 189 is the poem "Die Flucht der Stunden." This reference has already been noted by Patsch, "Zur Frühgeschichte der romantischen Hermeneutik," p. 242, n. 36. TRANS.: A textual correction has been noted.

25. Cf. Morus, Super hermeneutica, 1: 266-67; Ernesti, Institutio, pt. I, sec. 1, chap. 2, §8.

26. Cf. Morus, Super hermeneutica, 1: 264; Ernesti, Institutio, pt. I, sec. 1, chap. 2, §5.

27. Against both Morus, Super hermeneutica, 1: 271-73 and Ernesti, Institutio, pt. I, sec. 1, chap. 2, §14, who combined the concepts of synonyms and figurative expressions. TRANS.: Textual corrections have been noted.

28. Here the previously noted example from the New Testament, Gal. 1:6, is discussed further.

29. The example is from Gal. 1:16.

30. Cf. Ernesti, Institutio, pt. I, sec. 1, chap. 1, §§20-23.

31. Against Morus, Super hermeneutica, 1: 42, where it reads: "In poetry, tela solis signify radios solis, commae arborum are folia, so that tela and comae have different notions [alias notiones].

32. Discussed here is the example petere aliquem and ab aliquo, which upon closer determination occurs in the first or the second form; cf. Aphorism 93, p. 55 above.

33. The comparison between the Greek term πίστις and the Latin fides refers to Morus explanation (Super hermeneutica, 1:43) of Tit. 2:10.

34. See James Harris, Hermes oder philosophische Untersuchung über die Allgemeine Grammatik, trans.

Christian G. Ewerbeck, with notes and essays by Friedrich
A. Wolf and the translator, vol. 1 (Halle, 1788); 1st
English ed. (London, 1751). On the theory of verbs, cf.
pp. 143ff. The citation here has been noted by Patsch,
"Zur Frühgeschichte der romantischen Hermeneutik," pp.
471-72. TRANS.: A textual correction has been noted.

35. Cf. Aphorism 76, p. 53 above. TRANS.: A textual
correction has been noted.

36. Cf. Morus, Super hermeneutica, 1: 84-110, esp.
pp. 98-105, and Ernesti, Institutio, pt. 1, sec. 2, chap.
1, §§4-8.

37. Cf. Morus, Super hermeneutica, 1: 104-5.

38. TRANS.: A textual correction has been noted.

39. See Plato, Symposium, 223d.

40. See Theodor F. Stange, Theologische Symmikta
(Halle, 1805), 3: 122-30. A criticism of Stange's explanation of this passage similar to the one given here is
found in the review of his collected essays in the
Jenaischen Allgemeinen Literatur-Zeitung, on the page
cited by Schleiermacher. (TRANS.: A textual correction
has been noted.)

41. Cf. Ernesti, Institutio, pt. 1, sec. 2, chap. 1,
§17.

42. Cf. Ibid., §16, and Morus, Super hermeneutica,
1: 132-33.

43. It is not known to which place in Hugo Grotius'
work Schleiermacher is referring.

44. TRANS.: A textual correction has been noted.

45. See pp. 61, 63, 64, 95, 110, 112, 116, 153-54,
158-59, 175 and 222. (See Patsch, "Zur Frühgeschichte der
romantischen Hermeneutik," p. 466, n. 142.

46. Kimmerle and Patsch add the following marginal
note by Schleiermacher: "Plutarch adversus Colotem, III,
5 . . Stobäus 206 Physica, p. 264 political purpose, p.
347 melancholy, p. 325 contradiction 407 and 441 Expansion [Verbreitung] presupposed Twofold theoretical and
metaphorical translation is the separation of the two."
The Plutarch text comes from the Moralia. It seems that
the other citations refer to Ioannes Stobäus, Eclogarum
physicarum et ethicarum libri duo. The edition used by
Schleiermacher cannot be identified. The two texts are of
hermeneutical significance in that they are important
sources for the history of ancient philosophy.

47. From this point on the text evidently dates from
March, 1810.

48. According to Patsch, "Zur Frühgeschichte der
romantischen Hermeneutik," p. 461, this formulation of the
famous hermeneutical formula refers to Kant's Critique of

<u>Pure Reason</u>, ed. A, p. 318; ed. B, p. 370. Cf. Ms. 2,
n. 4 below; Ms. 3, nn. 12 and 15; Ms. 5, n. 26; and also,
Ms. 3', p. 156 and the note cited there.

MANUSCRIPT 1'

49. See Johann Wolfgang von Goethe, <u>Claudine von
Villa Bella</u>, first draft of 1776, 5: 389-90. The second
draft of this drama, dating from Goethe's trip to Rome,
(1787-88), no longer contains these verses. TRANS.: A
textual correction has been noted.

50. TRANS.: A textual correction has been noted.

51. See Plato, <u>Republik</u>, in 10 Books, trans. F. K.
Wolf, (vol. 1, Altona, 1799), pp. 129-30. Wolf assumes
that the subject of the passage (ἐκεῖνος) does not change.
TRANS.: A textual correction has been noted.

MANUSCRIPTS 2 AND 2'

1. For his criticism of Ernesti, <u>Institutio</u>, see
pp. 41-42 and pp. 43-46. Schleiermacher finds that the
rules given in §§4-5 of the Prol. "collide."

2. Cf. Aphorism 119, p. 59 and Aphorism 1, p. 41.

3. Cf. Aphorism 3, p. 41.

4. According to Patsch in "<u>Zur Frühgeschichte der
romantischen Hermeneutik</u>," this formulation of the chief
principle of hermeneutics is to be understood to come from
Friedrich Schlegel; see <u>Athenaüm</u> (Berlin, 1798), 1: 299.
Cf. Ms. 1, n. 48 above.

5. Against Ernesti's distinction between one sense
[<u>Sinn</u>] (<u>sensus</u>) and several meanings [<u>Bedeutungen</u>] (<u>sig-
nificationes</u>); see Ms. 1, nn. 8 and 9 above.

6. The Latin example is taken from Morus, <u>Super
hermeneutica</u>, 1: 260-61. See also Ms. 1, n. 12 above.
TRANS.: A textual correction has been noted.

7. The Latin example is taken from Morus, <u>Super
hermeneutica</u>, 1: 42. See also Ms. 1, n. 31 above.

8. Gulielmus Budaeus, <u>Commentarii linguage graecae</u>
(Paris, 1529; Coloniae, 1530, and elsewhere. Cf. also
Budaeus' <u>Lexicon graeco-latinum seu Thesaurus linguae
graecae</u> (Geneva, 1554). TRANS.: A textual correction has
been noted.

9. The Latin example comes from Morus. See also
Ms. 1, n. 32 above.

10. The collection of "other aids" corresponds to
<u>rationales subsidiariae</u> given by Ernesti, <u>Institutio</u>

pt. I, sec. 2, chap. 2, and by Morus, Super hermeneutica,
1: 148-94.

11.   Cf. this treatment of the use of parallel passages with the detailed theory in Morus, Super hermeneutica, 1: 16-17, 84-110. See also Ms. 1, nn. 6 and 36
above.

12.   TRANS.: The notation [3] has been added by the
translators in order to clarify the organization of the
outline.

13.   Ernesti had already objected to taking too many
passages as emphases without sufficient grammatical evidence (Institutio, pt. I, sec. 2, chap. 5, §§1-2). He rejected the theory of literal interpretation advocated by
both orthodoxy and pietism in the seventeenth and eighteenth centuries, criticizing as "fanatics" those who
maintained a special hermeneutical status for the biblical
texts (I, 1, 1, §16). Nevertheless, he states that these
texts were written by θεόπνευστοί [inspired writers] (I,
1, 1, §23). Although he admits that there are many figurative expressions in the Bible, he warns against devi-
ating from the general principles of interpretation "too
readily," i.e., without sufficient and necessary evidence
(I, 2, 4, §§2-4).

14.   For the hermeneutical significance of sensus
communis compare Morus, Super hermeneutica, 1: 185-91. In
this context both experientia and historia are mentioned
as aids for grasping the usus loquendi (p. 186).

15.   On the theory of analogia doctrinae, esp. the
analogia fidei, compare Ernesti, Interpretis, pt. I, sec.
1, chap. 1, §19; I, 2, 2, §15, and I, 2, 3, §§24 and 33-
35. This theory, which had played a central role in the
hermeneutics of orthodox Protestanism and was the foundation for dogmatic interpretation, goes back to Matthias
Flacius Illyricus, Clavis scripturae sacrae (1567); see in
the 2d ed. (Jena, 1674), esp. pt. I, 36 and pt. 2, 12.
From this theory of interpretation, including even
Ernesti's formulation of it (see Ms. 2, n. 13 above), it
followed that only apparent contradictions could be found
in the Scriptures (Ernesti, Institutio, I, 1, 1, §23).
This view affects the theory for eliminating ἐναντιοψανῶν
[apparent contradictions] (I, 2, 6).

16.   TRANS.: A textual correction has been noted.

17.   Following Ernesti, Morus distinguishes species
repugnantiae which occur 1) in dogmatic passages (Super
hermeneutica, 2: 8) and in historical passages (2: 22).

18.   In the chapter on "apparent contradictions"
Morus also deals with the question of the hermeneutical
significance of gospel harmonies (Super hermeneutica, 2:
34-43), i.e., presentations of the life and work of Jesus
which are compiled from the four biblical gospels and contain no contradictions.

MANUSCRIPT 2'

19. TRANS.: A textual correction has been noted.

20. TRANS.: The organization of the outline is unclear. It has been rendered as given in Kimmerle's edition.

MANUSCRIPTS 3 AND 3'

1. Schleiermacher refers here to Friedrich Ast, Grundlinien der Grammatik, Hermeneutik und Kritik (Landshut, 1808) and to Friedrich August Wolf, Darstellung der Altertumswissenschaft nach Begriff, Umfang, Zweck und Wert in Museum der Altertumswissenschaft, ed. F. A. Wolf and Philip Buttmann (Berlin, 1807), 1: 1ff.

2. Cf. Christian Wolff, Vernünfftige Gedanken von den Kräfften des menschlichen Verstandes und ihrem richtigen Gebrauche in der Erkäntnis der Wahrheit (Halle, 1713), esp. chaps. 10-12 (in the Latin ed., Philosophia rationalis sive Logica, methodo scientifica petractata et ad usum scientiarum atque vitae aptata [Frankfurt and Leipzig, 1728], pt. 2, sec. 3, Kant's inclusion of logic as a part of transcendental philosophy brought about this altered relationship between logic and hermeneutics.

3. J. A. Turrentinus first called for a general hermeneutics in the sense of applying general philological-historical methods to the Holy Scriptures (De sacra scripturae interpretandae methodo tractatus bipartitus, 1728). The work of J. S. Semler gave widespread importance to such efforts (see, esp. Abhandlung von freier Untersuchung des Canon, 4 parts, 1771-75). On the opposite side were orthodox and pietistic hermeneutics represented by W. Franz (De interpretatione sacrae scripturae, 1619); S. Glassius (Philologica sacra, 1623ff) and J. J. Rambach (Institutiones hermeneuticae sacrae, 1724; 6th ed., 1764) which presupposed an "immediate illumination" for the interpretation of the Holy Scriptures. In this "conflict" Ernesti and Morus took a "mediating position," but they emphasized the basic necessity of a "universal interpretation" (interpretatio universa).

4. The "allegorical sense" [sensus allegoricus] played a major role in the hermeneutical tradition for the explanation of contradictory or difficult passages as well as increasing the significance of everyday and trivial statements in the Bible. After Luther had given priority to the literal and tropological senses over the anagogical and especially the allegorical senses (see Karl Holl, Gesammelte Aufsätze, Vol. I: Luther, 5th ed. [Tübingen, 1927], p. 546, Protestant hermeneutics sought to limit allegorical interpretation as much as possible. The two parables mentioned as examples are found in Mk. 4:1-20 and Lk. 16:19-31.

5. Here Ernesti's objection to using allegorical interpretation too frequently is criticized; cf. Ernesti, Institutio, pt. I, sec. 1, chap. 1, §§2 and 9.

6. On dogmatic interpretation see Ms. 2, n. 15 above; on allegorical interpretation see n. 5 above; and on the question of the significance of the Scriptures see Ms. 2, n. 14 above.

7. On the doctrine of inspiration in Protestant hermeneutics see Ms. 2, nn. 14 and 15 above.

8. See the references in n. 7 above, which apply to the note of 1828 as well as to the 1819 text.

9. The Cabbalistic interpretations of the Jewish Scriptures made extensive use of allegorical methods of interpretation (cf. n. 4 above).

10. On the special application of hermeneutics to ancient and foreign languages see Ernesti, Institutio, pt. I, sec. 2, chap. 1.

11. On the history of theological hermeneutics compare Gerhard Ebeling, Evangelsiche Evangelienauslegung (Munich, 1942; on the history of juristic hermeneutics see Emilio Betti, Teoria generale della interpretatione, 2 vols. (Milan, 1955); German ed.: Allgemeine Auslegungslehre als Methodik der Geisteswissenschaften.

12. This formulation of the hermeneutical principle is a reflection of Schlegel's view (see Ms. 2, n. 4 above), but it is now developed from the center of Schleiermacher's conception. Cf. the references to the other passages that deal with this hermeneutical principle cited in Ms. 1, n. 48.

13. Cf. Ernesti's distinction between sensus and significatio (Institutio, pt. I, sec. 1, chap. 1, §§1-5) that is criticized by Morus. Morus maintains that a particular word has a meaning (significatio), but sensum nunc recte ponemus in notione rei expressae integra dictione (Super hermeneutica, 1: 28 and 55). The definitions were made more precise by Eichstaedt, the editor of Morus' lectures, by reference to the special essay of Morus, De discrimine sensus et significationis (Super hermeneutica, 1: 56-64).

14. Ernesti (Institutio, Prol., §§2 and 6) had already noted that interpretation required "in addition to knowledge, judgment, and zeal, a certain measure of talent [quandam ingenii felicitas] or even skill (εὐφυΐα) [solertia]. This led Morus to claim that interpretation be characterized not only as a "discriminating judgment (subtilitas) or a "faculty" (facultas), but as an art (Super hermeneutica, 1: 6). Cf. Ernesti, Institutio, Prol., §5, in which it is stated that "difficultatis intelligendi, earumque caussas, ex arte animadvertere."

15. The hermeneutical principle (see Ms. 1, n. 48 above) is here considered in relation to the grammatical method of interpretation.

16. The Latin example comes from Morus, Super hermeneutica, 1: 42 (cf. Ms. 1, n. 31 above).

17. "Creeping plant" is a translation of Morus' example, planta serpens (see Ms. 1, p. 46 and Ms. 2, p. 72 above).

18. Against Morus, Super hermeneutica, 1: 208-9.

19. TRANS.: Schleiermacher's outline here is unclear, and the text has been outlined by the translators.

20. The emphasis on the philological viewpoint over the dogmatic had been already prepared for by Ernesti (see Ms. 2, n. 13 above).

21. Against Ernesti, Institutio, pt. I, sec. 2, chap. 4, §4.

22. Cf. Ms. 2, n. 15 above.

23. This rule was conditioned by the Lutheran doctrine of sola scriptura which was originally directed against an explanation from tradition. The hermeneutical formula goes back to Flacius, Clavis scripturae sacrae, pt. 2, sp. 7, 60 and 694.

24. This first maxim forms a counter-statement in rationalistic biblical interpretation to that represented in pietistic hermeneutics: "take as much emphatically as possible" (soviel als möglich emphatisch zu nehmen). Cf. J. J. Rambach, Institutiones hermeneuticae sacra (1724).

25. Cf., e.g., in the Compendium theologiae dogmaticae by Christian F. Sartorius (Tübingen, 1777), chap. 8: De illuminatione, regeneratione, conversione, poenitentia et fide (pp. 230-69).

26. The conflict over Homer was sparked by F. A. Wolf, Prolegomena ad Homerum (Halle, 1794), republished as an introduction to his edition of Homer (Halle, 1795). In this piece Wolf advances the thesis that the works traditionally ascribed to Homer (the Iliad and the Odyssey) originated in six different eras and represent the work of several authors. Schleiermacher is referring to the three ancient tragedians, Aeschylus, Sophocles, and Euripedes.

MANUSCRIPT 3'

27. TRANS.: The subtitle is Application of Knowledge about the Author's Distinctiveness to Interpretation.

28. Cf. Ms. 1, n. 48 above.

29. TRANS.: Schleiermacher's outline is unclear and the text has been outlined by the translators.

MANUSCRIPT 4

1. Wolf treated the special problem of the <u>Iliad</u> in the Foreword to his work, in connection with the general introduction to the edition as a whole. J. S. Vater and W. M. L. de Wette almost simultaneously discovered that the Pentateuch and the book of Joshua were collections of texts derived from different traditions. While Vater first published this view (<u>Commentar über den Pentateuch</u>, Part 3, Halle 1805, pp. 391ff.: <u>Abhandlung über Moses und die Verfasser des Pentateuch</u>); de Wette developed it and brought it to prominence (<u>Beiträge zur Einleitung ins Alte Testament</u>, 2 vols. (Halle, 1806-7).

2. TRANS.: The brackets here and below are present in the German text.

MANUSCRIPT 5: THE ACADEMY ADDRESSES

The First Address

1. The editor of the Addresses has written in the margin: "Read in the plenary session on August 13, 1829--Jonas." On the different datings from Schleiermacher and Jonas cf. Kimmerle's Introduction, pp. 24-25 above.

2. In the history of Protestant theology since Flacius, <u>Clavis scripturae sacrae</u> (see Ms. 2, n. 15 above), hermeneutical texts were published again and again (see Ms. 3, n. 3 above).

3. G. G. Fülleborn, <u>Encyclopaedia philologica</u> (Bratislava, 1798). Schleiermacher refers here to the 2d edition, ed. D. J. S. Kaulfuss (Bratislava, 1805). See esp. <u>Pars prima</u>: I. <u>Grammatica</u>, II. <u>Critica</u>, III. <u>Hermeneutica</u>. See also Ms. 2, n. 15 above.

4. The essay by Wolf opened the journal <u>Museum der Alterthums-Wissenschaft</u>, ed. F. A. Wolf and Philip Buttmann, p. 79, n. 1.

5. See Ast, <u>Grundlinien</u>, pp. iii-viii.

6. See Wolf, <u>Darstellung</u>, pp. 3-6.

7. Ibid., pp. 34-41. The term 'organon' is found on p. 35.

8. In "<u>Zur Frühgeschichte der romantischen Hermeneutik</u>," p. 438, n. 21, Patsch has noted that Schleiermacher evidently was not familiar with the Ast's <u>Grundriss der Philologie</u>, which was published in Landshut in 1808, the same year as the <u>Grundlinien</u>.

9. In his <u>Brief Outline of Theology</u> (1811; 2d ed., 1830), Schleiermacher drafted a theological encyclopedia (cf. 2d ed., Intro., §20). In addition to hermeneutics, Schleiermacher presents higher and lower criticism, know-

ledge of languages, and mastery of the historical milieu
as the organon of "exegetical theology," which is itself
of fundamental importance for theology as a whole. (Cf.
2d ed., §§110-46).

10. Ast, Grundlinien, pp. 167-71.

11. Wolf, Darstellung, p. 37.

12. Ibid.

13. Ast, Grundlinien, pp. 167-68.

14. See Wolf, Darstellung, pp. 34-35; Ast, Grundlinien, pp. 173-74.

15. See Wolf, Darstellung, p. 37.

16. According to Patsch, "Zur Frühgeschichte der
romantischen Hermeneutik," Schleiermacher is referring to
Friedrich Schlegel, who died January 12, 1829; see
Athenäum, Berlin, 1798, (1: 197-98).

17. See Wolf, Darstellung, pp. 240-41.

18. See Plato, Ion, 530c-531d.

19. See n. 8 above.

20. Wolf, Darstellung, pp. 42-44.

21. Cf. Ibid., pp. 36-37.

22. Ibid., pp. 42-44.

23. Ibid.

24. Ibid.

25. Ibid., p. 37.

26. Here the basic hermeneutical principle of the
"psychological" interpretation of "composition" is interpreted as an inner "process." (See also Ms. 1, n. 48
above).

27. Ast, Grundlinien, pp. 171-72.

The Second Address

28. See Ernesti, Institutio, pt. I, sec. 1, chap. 1,
§§4-5.

29. Ast, Grundlinien, pp. 186-87.

30. See p. 181 above and n. 14 cited there.

31. See Plato, Phaedrus 276d and 277c-278b.

32. Wolf, Darstellung, pp. 42-44.

33. Ast, Grundlinien, pp. 178-184.

34. Ibid., pp. 171, 176-77, 182.

35. Ibid., pp. 188-90.

36.   Ibid., p. 177.

37.   Ibid., pp. 191-92.

38.   Ibid., pp. 184-85. From the beginning Schleiermacher criticized the distinction between understanding
[intelligere] and interpretation, esp. explanation [expli-
care]. 1. The distinction goes back to Augustine, De
Doctrina Christiana (396/426). In Books 1-3 Augustine
deals with understanding the teaching [Lehre] of Christianity and in Book 4 he deals with the restatement
[Wiedergabe] of what has been understood. This distinction was generally accepted until Wolf (Darstellung, p.
37) and Schleiermacher.

39.   Wolf, Darstellung, p. 37.

40.   Ast, Grundlinien, pp. 194-95.

41.   Wolf, Darstellung, p. 37.

42.   The extension of grammatical interpretation to
dogmatic interpretation (see Ms. 2, n. 15 above) and allegorical interpretation (see Ms. 3, n. 4 above) was developed by the humanistically educated theologian Hugo
Grotius and, on the Catholic side, Richard Simon. In
these, the historical context for interpretation was included from the beginning. One can speak of grammatical-
historical interpretation in the sense of a strict application of historical methods and of an opposition to dogmatic and allegorical interpretations with J. S. Semler
(cf. Ms. 3, n. 3 above). Schleiermacher wants to overcome
the frontal opposition between different kinds of interpretation.

43.   Ast, Grundlinien, pp. 196-97.

44.   The idea of a "moral interpretation" is obvious
in enlightenment philosophy. It is introduced in Semler's
hermeneutics (cf., e.g., Abhandlung von freier Untersuchung des Canons, 1:23). Kant advances it in Die
Religion innerhalb der Grenzen der blossen Vernunft
2d ed. (Königsberg, 1794), p. 161; cf. Ms. 3, n. 48 above.
(The reference to this passage was noted by H. G. Gadamer.) The "inventor" of panharmonic interpretation cannot
be identified.

MANUSCRIPT 6

1.   Reference is made to Ast, Grundlinien and Wolf,
Darstellung.

2.   See Ms. 2, n. 13 above.

3.   See Aphorism 75, p. 53 above and n. 31 cited
there, as well as Ms. 2, p. 74 above.

4.   S. S. C. Dittmann, Predigten zur Beförderung der
häuslichen Tugenden (Königsberg, 1798). (?)

5. TRANS.: A textual correction of the Greek has been noted.

6. See An Historical View of Christianity; containing select passages from Scripture with a commentary by the late Edward Gibbon and notes by the late Lord Viscount Bolingbroke, Monsieur de Voltaire and others (London, 1806).

AFTERWORD OF 1968

1. The notebooks by students attending Schleiermacher's lectures on hermeneutics are to be found in the Literaturarchiv der Deutschen Akademie der Wissenschaften in Berlin. They include: "Hermeneutik nach Schleiermacher, z. T. in Auszügen im Sommer 1822" by Saunier-Schirmer; "Hermeneutik und Kritik nach den Vortragen des Herrn Prof. Dr. Schleiermacher, WS 1826-27" by I. Braune; "Schleiermacher Hermeneutik und Kritik," incomplete from the winter semester of 1828-29 (?) by Spanenberg (?); "Hermeneutik nach dem Vortrage des H. Dr. Schleiermacher, Sommer, 1829" by L. Jonas, and "Die Hermeneutik und die Kritik von 1832-33" by F. Lücke.

2. Gadamer, Wahrheit und Methode.

3. Ibid., p. 174, n. 2 and p. 180, n. 1.

4. Wolfhart Pannenberg, ["Rezension"], Monatsschrift für Pastoraltheologie 49 (1960): 447. Pannenberg comes to the same judgment in his essay "Hermeneutik und Universalgeschichte," Zeitschrift für Theologie und Kirche 60 (1963): 90-121; English trans.: "Hermeneutics and Universal History," trans. Paul J. Achtemeier, in Journal for Theology and the Church, ed. Robert W. Funk, vol. 4: History and Hermeneutic (New York: Harper and Row, 1967), pp. 122-52.

5. Wilhelm Dilthey, Gesammelte Schriften, vol. 14, 1: Leben Schleiermachers, ed. Martin Redeker (Göttingen: Vandenhoeck und Ruprecht, 1966).

6. Hans Georg Geyer, "Rezension," Zeitschrift für Kirchengeschichte 2 (1961): 197-200.

7. Heinz Kimmerle, "Das Verhältnis Schleiermachers zum Transcendental Idealismus," Kant-Studien 51 (1959-60): 410-26; idem, Hermeneutische Theorie oder ontologische Hermeneutik," Zeitschrift für Theologie und Kirche 59 (1962): 114-30; English trans.: "Hermeneutical Theory or Ontological Hermeneutics," trans. Friedrich Seifert, in Journal for Theology and Church, 4: 107-21; idem, "Metahermeneutik, Applikation, hermeneutische Sprachbildung," Zeitschrift für Theologie und Kirche 61 (1964): 221-35; and idem, Sprachfähigkeit und Weltbewaltigung," Philosophisches Jahrbuch 73 (1965-66): 356-71.

8. Patsch, "Zur Frühgeschichte der romantischen Hermeneutik," pp. 434-72.

9. Körner, "Friedrich Schlegel's 'Philosophie der Philologie,'" Logos 17 (1928): 1-72.

10. Patsch, "Zur Frühgeschichte der romantischen Hermeneutik," p. 464.

11. Dilthey, Gesammelte Schriften, 14, 2: 595-787; cf. pp. lxxxii-iii.

12. The beginning of this essay was published in 1893 by Dilthey as part of his essay "Das System der Geisteswissenschaften in 17. Jahrhundert" in Archiv für Geschichte der Philosophie (see Dilthey, Gesammelte Schriften, 2: 115ff.

13. See Dilthey, "Die Entstehung der Hermeneutik," pp. 317-31.

14. Dilthey, Gesammelte Schriften, 14,2: 688.

15. Ibid., pp. 688-89; cf. p. 691, n. 1.